Start Your Own

MAIL ORDER

Business

"…good addition to practical business collections."

Booklist

"…practical recommendations."

Denver Business Journal

"…tries to answer every question a fledgling entrepreneur might have…"

Orange County Register

Start Your Own

MAIL ORDER

Business

PRENTICE HALL
Englewood Cliffs, New Jersey 07632

Printed in the United States of America

10 9 8 7 6 5 4 3 2 1

ISBN 0-13-603051-3

This publication is designed to provide accurate and authoritative information in regard to the subject matter covered. It is sold with the understanding that the publisher is not engaged in rendering legal, accounting, or other professional service. If legal advice or other expert assistance is required, the services of a competent professional person should be sought.

. . . From the Declaration of Principles jointly adopted by a Committee of the American Bar Association and a Committee of Publishers and Associations.

ATTENTION: CORPORATIONS AND SCHOOLS

Prentice Hall books are available at quantity discounts with bulk purchase for educational, business, or sales promotional use. For information, please write to: Prentice Hall Career & Personal Development Special Sales, 113 Sylvan Avenue, Englewood Cliffs, NJ 07632. Please supply: title of book, ISBN number, quantity, how the book will be used, date needed.

PRENTICE HALL
Career & Personal Development
Englewood Cliffs, NJ 07632
A Simon & Schuster Company

On the World Wide Web at http://www.phdirect.com

Prentice Hall International (UK) Limited, *London*
Prentice Hall of Australia Pty. Limited, *Sydney*
Prentice Hall Canada, Inc., *Toronto*
Prentice Hall Hispanoamericana, S.A., *Mexico*
Prentice Hall of India Private Limited, *New Delhi*
Prentice Hall of Japan, Inc., *Tokyo*
Simon & Schuster Asia Pte. Ltd., *Singapore*
Editora Prentice Hall do Brasil, Ltda., *Rio de Janeiro*

CONTENTS

PREFACE

Start Your Own Mail Order Business is the result of many hours of in-depth research into the mail order industry. Our exclusive team of National Business Library's professional business writers has brought years of practical experience to this project, and we know that the information provided in this book will set you on the road to success.

Owning your own business can be the most exciting and rewarding venture you will ever experience. We talk of hundreds of small business owners who make comments like, "Doing something I really enjoy makes every new day a pleasure," or "If I had known I could be realizing this kind of income, rather than making my former boss wealthy, I would have started my own business years ago."

It's true! You'll never get rich working for someone else. By capitalizing on your experience, investing time and energy, and studying the proven techniques and business methods provided in this book, you will be well on the way to realizing your goals for success in your own venture. It takes courage to begin. Without a doubt, the first step is the hardest—and you have already taken it.

INTRODUCTION: THE $70 BILLION OPPORTUNITY

Last year more than 30 percent of the American population spent over $70 billion on items they purchased through mail order. And that doesn't include magazine subscriptions and orders placed with record and book clubs. It is estimated that mail-order shoppers spend an average of $25 per order, with items under $10 selling most often. People like the fun and convenience of shopping by mail and gladly pay for the opportunity to make purchases without leaving home.

There has never been a better time to jump on the mail-order bandwagon. It is predicted that sales will continue to grow at approximately 15 percent per year, as they have done every year over the past decade. It is not difficult to enter into this exciting and extremely profitable business. The main requirements are a salable product or line of products and a good marketing plan. The mail-order giants depend on repeat business for their growth. The best way to get customers to order again and again is to

1. Satisfy them the first time around
2. Stay in touch with them by consistently sending out material on new products or offers

The profit potential in the mail order business is limited only by your ability and desire to look for new products and market them. We have talked with single-product mail-order operators who are perfectly satisfied supplementing a day job income with $400 to $500 a month.

There are others who handle a number of products and make thousands of dollars every month, while the large mail-order houses realize gross income in the millions on an annual basis.

The choice is yours, which is another aspect that makes mail order such an attractive opportunity. You call all the shots and can basically dictate the amount of money you make. But beware: According to those we interviewed, once you get involved in the business, it is easy to become hooked! And once you are hooked on finding new products to promote, you can't help but increase your chances for profits!

This is an excellent business to start on a small scale. Basing the operation in your home with one or two products is an option that will only cost you a few hundred dollars. Your major expense at the onset will be for advertising. It is even possible to hold off on buying a large inventory of products until you have begun to receive orders, which will keep start-up costs low.

However, starting small does not preclude thinking big! If you are looking for long-term involvement in the business, the time to begin developing success habits is from day one. This means accepting responsibility in the following areas:

- ♦ Finding products that appeal to the general consumer's need

- ♦ Preparing creative, yet simple advertising material

- ♦ Developing an order system that is convenient and easy to use

- ♦ Maintaining product quality at all times

- ♦ Making "customer service" the phrase of the day...every day

If you use these basic guidelines in running your mail-order business, it is a good bet you will soon find yourself on the path to success.

1

THE GROWTH OF SMALL BUSINESS

The 1980s were referred to as America's "entrepreneurial era." In 1986, more than 750,000 new businesses were created in the United States. In 1989, more than a million new ventures were started nationwide–almost half of them by women–and the entrepreneurial era is continuing through the 1990s. The recession of the early 1990s compelled suddenly unemployed people to start their own businesses in order to survive. An upsurge in part-time businesses has also fueled entrepreneurism in the nineties, with people in search of extra income working on profitable ventures during their off-hours.

More and more people are opting to leave their 9-to-5 jobs and stop "making someone else rich" to focus their energies on building a successful business of their own. For these people, it is no longer enough to spend nearly three-quarters of their lives working in a dead-end job, putting up with petty office politics, unappreciative employers, and long commutes just to bring home headaches and a small paycheck.

Today, the number of individuals who are self-employed is at its highest level ever, and based on your interest in this book, it's quite possible that you'll be joining the ranks of small business owners in the near future. It may be simply a dream right now, but that's how these businesses start.

You can never be too young, too old, too busy, or too poor to start a business.

Starting and operating your own small business is one of the most exciting and satisfying challenges you can undertake. There are no limitations on income potential when you're investing time and energy in your own enterprise. With the practical information provided in this book and dedication to your business goals, your chances for success are excellent.

What Is a Small Business?

The majority of businesses in the United States today are classified as small businesses. The definitions of what constitutes a small business run the gamut from the size of the overall staff (typically under 100) to the amount of assets or sales volume. However, in this book, small business is defined as one that is independently owned and operated.

The major benefit of this type of business is that you have the ability to make decisions quickly and act on them immediately. What typically bogs down big business is the number of people involved in the decision-making process.

Other advantages include the fact that small businesses can provide personalized service to the community or the market they're serving and the owner has the freedom, independence, and control to operate exactly as he or she chooses.

It's important to remember, however, that most major corporations, from Ford Motor Company and McDonald's to Mary Kay Cosmetics, started out as small businesses—as dreams.

It was because of basic business sense and a willingness to learn and adapt as their companies grew that Henry Ford, Ray Kroc, and Mary Kay, and thousands like them, steered their dreams into monumental financial successes.

Whether your goal is to supplement an existing income and to operate a solely owned home-based business from your garage, kitchen table, or spare bedroom, or to start a business that involves raising substantial capital, finding and setting up a commercial

location, and hiring employees, you have the potential to enjoy an independent lifestyle that carries with it a number of rewards. And the rewards are as varied as the people who pursue them.

Entrepreneur
A person who undertakes an independent enterprise; one who has made the decision to go into business for him/herself.

Accepting the Challenge

Remember, these rewards do not come without hard work and the willingness to research and understand all facets of running your business. Many new businesses fail within the first few years.

Reasons given for the early demise of a small business range from lack of organization or management experience to undercapitalization, misunderstanding of the importance of advertising, inexperience in pricing products and services, lack of an overall business plan, improper hiring practices, and failure to meet the competition.

It isn't that someone purposely starts a business without having explored these areas. However, many times a person feels that his or her demonstrated expertise while in the employ of another can easily be transferred into a personal business. This is only partially true.

While it is imperative that you have these particular skills or talents—because selling them is what your ultimate success will be based on—it's equally important to understand how to sell them, to know exactly what your profit margin is, and what steps you need to take to ensure the continued growth of your business.

Sounds easy, right? It really can be. But like anything else worth doing, starting your own business means careful planning. For example, you wouldn't consider taking a month-long vacation without doing some serious planning to ensure that the house was taken care of while you were gone, that you had made reservations

for lodging, tours, and flights, and that you had converted your cash into traveler's checks.

There are so many aspects involved in running a business, it is vital to be prepared for any eventuality. Being prepared means being informed, so that when situations do arise, you know how to deal with them.

Is "Failure" Really Failure?

We have all heard stories about people who started their businesses on a shoestring and who became successful because of their sheer determination to make it work. It does happen, but these people are the exception rather than the rule, and in most cases have had experts standing behind them to give them guidance when problems came up. Others fail and, unfortunately, this often holds potential new business owners back. We hear and read about amazingly high figures related to so-called business failures.

According to a research project conducted by Albert Shapero, professor of the American Free Enterprise System at Ohio State University for many years, no one really knows the true failure rate of new business. The main reason for this is because there is not really a standard definition of "failure" in this case. He points out that a number of businesses close for a variety of reasons, many of which are not documented.

For example, in some cases the owners reach retirement age and have no one to pass the business along to; others shut down because the owners simply get bored; while still other entrepreneurs file a Chapter 11 bankruptcy, which basically gives them the opportunity to stay in business and continue operating under a court-approved plan, even though they become a statistic on the "failure" list.

The other extremely important aspect to consider when thinking about the benefits and risks of starting your own business is that having a business fail has never been a deterrent for true entrepreneurs. Many well-known business moguls failed at least once, and often more than once, before striking it rich.

Learning From Experience

In fact, almost anyone who has had a business fail will tell you that the experience was more valuable than anything they could have been taught in a business school and provided them with the knowledge they needed to start another venture successfully. This kind of determination is a valid qualification for self-employment and will pay off handsomely.

When you own your own business, you are responsible for everything. There will be times, such as when your accounts receivable are running sixty days late or the phone company puts the wrong number in your Yellow Pages listing, that returning to the 9-to-5 world will seem like a viable option.

This is where self-discipline, an unwavering belief in your product or service, and the determination to be your own boss will pull you through.

But, again, we can't stress enough the importance of planning, understanding basic business practices, being aware of consumer trends, and taking the time to develop, implement, and update goals to ensure success for your efforts.

What This Book Offers

This book is designed to provide you with the information you will need to start your mail order business, to offer techniques to help you with day-to-day operations, and to provide actual case histories of people just like you who had a dream and, through planning and determination, were able to turn that dream into a successful reality.

In addition to focusing on aspects of the mail order business, we cover such important business matters as

♦ Recognizing the entrepreneurial profile

♦ Taking our exclusive Entrepreneurial Quiz

♦ Finding the right audience for your business through easy marketing techniques

♦ Organizing for efficiency

♦ Recognizing legalities

- ♦ Addressing financial concerns
- ♦ Getting your home office up and running
- ♦ Charting your enterprise's growth

You will find specific how-to information on

- ♦ Advertising and promoting your business
- ♦ Finding capital
- ♦ Saving money on operating expenses
- ♦ Developing a simple bookkeeping system that will show you whether you're facing a financial crisis or realizing a profit

You're never too young, too old, too busy, or too poor to start a business. Owning your own business means taking advantage of our marvelous system of free enterprise. Earning a substantial living and, even better, realizing a profit for doing something you enjoy is the American dream come true.

The road to financial independence through self-employment is challenging and rewarding.

The opportunities for entrepreneurs have never been better. Armed with a solid product or service to sell, the determination to succeed and, most important, business know-how, there is nothing that can stand in your way.

Notes

Key Points

Personal Thoughts

Additional Research

2

THE ENTREPRENEURIAL PROFILE

Starting a business is one thing, making it work is another. We know that success in self-employment is largely the result of careful planning and an understanding of basic business techniques and formulas.

Start a business based on your expertise in a specific field and focus your involvement in an area that you thoroughly enjoy.

As many successful entrepreneurs claim, making money doing something you love is the best way to ensure a profitable future. It is always easier to address the inevitable business challenges that crop up when you are creating a product or providing a service that gives you a sense of pleasure and personal satisfaction.

Personality is a significant factor in determining what kind of business to get involved in, the way you will eventually set up the legal structure (sole proprietorship, partnership, etc.), and how you will run the business on a day-to-day basis. For example, if you are planning to start a business that is based on your artistic

or creative abilities, it is possible that your personality is not suited to the very important aspect of sales. But without strong selling abilities, there is a likelihood that your goal of distributing, for example, your hand-carved wooden boxes nationally will not come to fruition.

This isn't to say that you should decide against going into business for yourself. It simply indicates it would be in your best interest to join forces with someone who does have strong selling skills, who believes in the product as much as you do, and who will work with you toward a common goal.

On the other hand, if your personality is geared to working with people, it is a good idea to consider a business that will emphasize this ability, such as developing seminars or workshops based on your area of expertise, providing independent counseling or tutoring, or providing a service such as gift basket designing or desktop publishing, which depends on your interaction with people on a one-to-one or a group basis for success.

Research shows that in order to address the many and varied situations that arise in business ownership, the true entrepreneur should possess the following personality traits.

Ten Important Entrepreneurial Traits

1. Self-awareness	6. Decisiveness
2. Self-motivation	7. Experience
3. Courage	8. Knowledge
4. Confidence	9. Perseverance
5. Patience	10. Drive

1. ***Self-awareness.*** Know who you are, what you're good at, and what you like to do. Start a business that is based on your expertise in a specific field and focus your involvement in an area that you thoroughly enjoy.

2. ***Self-motivation.*** Also known as drive, self-motivation is one of the most important personality traits of successful

entrepreneurs. This is the characteristic that gets you going and keeps you moving when you are in business for yourself. It's what helps you to keep turning out those craft items, upgrading your technical skills, or developing new and improved promotional techniques when business is slow. It's what gives you the tenacity and confidence to call on a potential client even though you've heard "No" three times.

Self-motivation is also what helps you overcome the fears and concerns that inevitably arise when you own your own business. It is the main ingredient that has spurred on people who have achieved success despite drawbacks, such as minimal capital, lack of education, or limited experience.

People with a high degree of self-motivation see the greatest obstacles, such as learning a new aspect of business management, as a new and exciting challenge to overcome. If you've ever undertaken a project without fully understanding the mechanics involved in performing the task or knowing what the outcome would be, you were operating on self-motivation—the conviction that you would be able to learn whatever was needed to accomplish your goal.

And regardless of the outcome of the project, you undoubtedly gained more experience and knowledge than you had before, which only works to increase your sense of motivation to handle new challenges.

3. *Courage.* Courage or the willingness to take risks is a valuable trait when striving for success. A successful person might say something like: "I don't know how I did it; I just made a phone call and asked for the money I needed." It was more than luck that made it possible for this person to raise the needed capital to get a business off the ground; it was the willingness to take a chance and hope for a positive response to the request.

The owner of a small cabinet-refinishing business said, "I always figure that the worst thing that can happen is someone will say no, so it never hurts to try." In the game

of business, you must be willing to take chances. Even if you don't get exactly what you want every time, the odds are good that if you feel strongly about what you need, you will get it. But you have to ask!

4. **Confidence.** The age-old philosophy of positive thinking is a major step in the direction of success. By behaving as if you already are a success at what you do, it follows that you will be, and your customers will believe that you are successful, too. A confident attitude is one of the most appealing traits you can exhibit to prospective clients, for it lets them know that they will be getting the best their money can buy.

You have to accept whatever comes, and the important thing is that you meet it with courage and with the best you have to give.

Eleanor Roosevelt

5. **Patience.** When you own your own business, there will be times when you feel like the roof is caving in, especially when your suppliers seem to be taking their own sweet time in fulfilling an important order or when a customer's demands seem to be unrealistic. Although you may be able to hurry the supplier along, you must remember that your customers are always right, since they are the ones who will make or break your business.

If you are aware that patience is not your strong suit, develop a stop-gap exercise to use at times when coping is a definite necessity. Whether you count to ten before saying a word, visualize a pleasant scene, or repeat a secret phrase to yourself when tension is running high, it will be to your advantage.

6. **Decisiveness.** Business has been described as a process of making one fast decision after another. Often, a decision has to be made immediately, on the spur of the

moment. In those instances, you should go with your intuition and trust that you are doing the right thing.

However, if you are the type of person who prefers to analyze your options, weigh all the factors, and make decisions slowly, then that is what you must do. It will keep your confidence intact and ensure that you're taking the right action. Again, careful planning will help you predict many of the decision-making situations that arise in your business. As time goes by and you grow more comfortable in your role as business owner, you will undoubtedly find yourself making quicker decisions.

7. *Experience.* A primary reason some businesses fail within a few years of start-up is lack of business experience. Whether or not your experience is directly related to the business you are planning to start, it is a key component for growth.

If you feel you do not have enough business experience, there are several avenues you can take before starting your own enterprise. Returning to school for specialized courses is one consideration. Most community colleges and adult education facilities offer classes and seminars in business start-up and maintenance, and there are hundreds of home-study or correspondence courses that will, in many cases, give you official certification in your field.

However, your best solution is to take a job in the field you're interested in. By asking questions about all the aspects of the business, you will gain experience, get paid for learning, and find out whether this is really what you want to do before sinking money, time, and energy into the enterprise.

8. *Knowledge.* Experience in your field is invaluable, but it is not enough. You have a better chance of succeeding the more you know about such vital factors as business basics, the product or service that you want to sell, the industry you are entering, your competition, and the local, regional, state, and/or national markets. Do your homework.

9. *Perseverance.* One of the adages you will hear time and time again when talking to entrepreneurs is that perseverance is 90 percent of the battle to succeed.

 If you are like the majority of new small business owners, the entire staff and support system for your venture is probably *you.* Making a dream come true can be a lonely task, especially when you are just getting started, and ensuring that it works often means little rest or relaxation. You must be willing to persevere during the rough times, to hang in there during the slow periods, and to maintain your belief in your product or service—even when it seems like no one else in the world knows you exist. It has been written that through perseverance the snail reached the ark. So it is with success!

10. *Drive.* You must believe in your goal and be determined to succeed. The successful businessperson does not view obstacles or stumbling blocks as problems, but rather as challenges. To make your business a success, you need to be totally committed and willing to work long hours, especially in the beginning. If you do not have the time or commitment to dedicate to your dream, then you are better off working for someone else.

The Entrepreneurial *A* to *Z* Appraisal

Owning a business calls for the ability to handle different situations with confidence. The following self-appraisal quiz has no right or wrong answers. It is designed to help you determine certain personality traits, attitudes, and qualifications that will benefit you in your venture. Upon completion, use the appraisal as a starting point for discussions with friends and family members about your business profile. Acknowledging your strong and weak points will help you prepare for your role as an entrepreneur.

Entrepreneurial Quiz

Use the letter *S* for strong or *N* for needs improvement beside the characteristics listed below. Give yourself sufficient time to analyze each trait.

Achievement: I have a strong desire to be successful in my chosen business venture. _____

Belief: I have faith in myself and the service or product I am specializing in to build my business. _____

Creativity: I am able to address situations in imaginative and innovative ways to reach my goals. _____

Discipline: I am self-motivated and can handle necessary tasks, whether or not I enjoy them. _____

Efficient: I am organized and can arrange my priorities or change my work methods as needed for maximum production. _____

Friendly: I am genuinely interested in people and enjoy my interactions with them on a day-to-day basis. _____

Goal Oriented: I have a tendency to set my sights on preset goals and will work hard toward achieving them. _____

Health Conscious: I am aware of my physical abilities and have the insight to work smart in order to preserve my health. _____

Independent: I am able to work alone, if necessary, and am willing to be responsible for my own actions. _____

Judgment: My conclusions about people or situations are generally accurate. _____

Knowledge: I have solid experience in my field and have spent enough time in a professional business setting to know the ropes. _____

Leadership: I am able to direct people effectively while instilling confidence and loyalty. _____

Maturity: I am willing to work toward long-term goals and do not get upset by the inevitable minor setbacks. _____

Networking: I am willing to develop associations with other entrepreneurs for professional support in my venture. _____

Optimism: I am able to see what is right about a situation and to explore its potential to the fullest. _____

Positive Attitude: I am convinced that I can accomplish anything I set my mind to, and rarely entertain negative thoughts. _____

Questioning: I am not afraid to ask questions to get the information I need to expand my knowledge. _____

Resourceful: I am able to find ways to accomplish just about any task I must do. _____

Sales Ability: I can present information about myself and/or my business in a convincing yet honest manner. _____

Tolerance: I am able to handle stressful situations with a positive and realistic attitude. _____

Undaunted Spirit: I am unafraid of the unknown. In fact, I enjoy a challenge and accept the consequences of my actions. _____

Venturesome: I am not afraid of hard work to reach my goals and enjoy finding new, positive ways to handle troublesome situations. _____

Well Balanced: I generally maintain a sense of humor when things don't work out as expected. _____

eXpressive: I am able to express ideas and feelings clearly and logically, both orally and in written form. _____

Youthful Nature: I am capable of tackling work with enthusiasm and a high level of energy.

Zest: I look forward to enjoying my business, the people I will be dealing with, and the resulting fruits of my labor.

Scoring

Although this is merely a tool to provide you with information about your entrepreneurial profile, there are immediate clues to your future as a business owner in the responses you have given.

Add up your number of _S_ responses and read the following interpretation that corresponds to the number you scored.

- ♦ 15+: There is a good possibility that you have been in-volved in your own business in the past or, at least, have worked in a managerial capacity for someone else. You have the positive personality traits required to be a suc-cessful business owner.

- ♦ 8-14: You are basically a positive and directed person and should not have any problem with improving certain areas to increase your personal business success potential.

- ♦ 0-7: This is an indication that finding a complementary business partner who can support your goals may be an option worth considering.

Notes

Key Points

Personal Thoughts

Additional Research

3

Starting a Mail Order Business

One of the most lucrative areas for entrepreneurial endeavor is mail order. Unlike many other small businesses, mail order offers you a high profit potential with low start-up capital requirements that can generate substantial income in short order.

There are a number of advantages that set mail order apart from other business ventures. For one thing, the public is conditioned to appreciate mail order merchandising. Giant corporations like L.L. Bean and Spiegel's, which are both billion-dollar companies, use the mail to sell an endless variety of goods to Americans all over the world. Countless smaller companies provide mail order consumers with just about anything they could possibly want.

The Income Picture

As with many businesses, the income you generate in mail order depends entirely on effort. For example, if you just sell one product working only a few hours a week out of your home, you might augment your monthly income by several hundred dollars.

On the other hand, some of the most successful one-person operations that have outgrown living rooms earn as much as $70,000 a year. Then, of course, there are phenomena, such as Pet Rocks, that earn their creators millions. And who isn't familiar

Overview of the Mail Order Business

This is a medium-risk business with solid profit potential. The mail order industry is expected to grow steadily over the next decade. Success depends on choosing and promoting unique products at a fair price.

"Shoestring" Start-up Investment:	$200
Average Start-up Investment: (Working from a home office)	$5,000
High Start-up Investment: (Producing a color catalog)	$75,000
Break-even Point:	Six months to two years
Average Annual Gross Revenues:	$20,000 to $75,000
Potential Annual Gross Revenues:	$150,000

with such multimillion-dollar companies as Currents, Fingerhut, L.L. Bean, and Hanover House?

Something to consider as you formulate your start-up plan is how you want your business to grow. Ask yourself these important questions.

1. If your profit is directly proportional to your sales volume, how much must you let your sales expand to realize as much profit as you can?

2. If starting on a part-time basis, do you want this to be a full-time endeavor at some point down the road?

3. Do you have the capability to support the growth you envision?

4. Will the market support the direction in which you want to grow?

It is important to realize that most businesses experience peaks and valleys that are relative to the ups and downs of their respective industries. Here the news is bright, as mail order offers

excellent long-term growth potential because the industry itself can only get bigger.

Steady Future

Over $70 billion is spent every year on mail-order items–a figure that does not even account for magazine subscriptions or book and record clubs! And it's obvious that the public enjoys shopping by mail more than ever, because sales have been increasing steadily between 10 and 25 percent every year over the past decade.

The Census Bureau estimates that the U.S. population will rise to 300 million people by the year 2000. That means about 87 million more folks than there are today, and all of them are potential mail-order shoppers.

How do all those people spend their mail-order dollars? While pricing varies widely, it is estimated that mail-order shoppers spend an average of $25 per order, with items under $10 selling most often. That's valuable information when you think about pricing your products. A lot of people will spend $5, $10, even $20 for something they think is a good value.

But higher-priced items–$50, $75, and up–are carefully considered before being purchased. The best way to be sure you get a slice of the ever-growing billion-dollar mail-order pie is to look ahead, then develop a sound pricing policy and business plan, both of which are discussed in the chapters ahead.

Analyzing Profit Potential

At this point, it is a good idea to do a cost/benefit analysis, which will kill two birds with one stone. Creating a basic costs-and-profits picture is not only an absolute necessity before you decide to commit to your venture, but doing so will also help you focus on some of the general information. While doing this, keep in mind that your business is basically concerned with three financial components: cost (of your product), overhead (advertising, printing, etc.), and profit (what you take to the bank).

What can you sell through mail order? A better question is what can't you sell through mail order? Anything, from aardvark pillows to zwieback crackers is fair game, and, in fact, the more unique, the better!

First, determine your product and its price. Let's say that for years you've made earrings as a hobby, selling your crafts at bazaars, flea markets, and even a couple of local retail outlets. Thus far, you've sold your product for $5 a pair, and that seems to be a reasonable price. It costs you $3 in materials, time, and packaging per pair and, since there are no other expenses because you work at home, you see a clear $2 profit on each pair sold.

Taking your earrings into the mail order market changes all that. Now you have to take into account additional costs such as advertising and postage, which, when computed against your projected sales, will tell you approximately what kind of gross profits you can expect. You'll need to come up with a new selling price that reflects these extra costs, then project figures for volume of say 500 orders, 1,000 orders, and 5,000 orders.

Your total costs will be determined by the product—its production, inventory, and shipping requirements—as well as where you choose to base the business. Let's say you're going to start out at home.

All the major "office" expenses are automatically taken care of, so the primary expenses for you at start-up will be for inventory, advertising, and shipping. Even then, you can often hold off on inventory and shipping expenses until orders start coming in and you have a positive cash flow.

Here's the picture so far, reflecting what things might look like after your first mailing:

Costs			
	500	1,000	5,000
Materials @ $3/pr.	$1,500	$3,000	$15,000
Postage @ $.50/pc.	250	500	2,500
Envelopes @ $.06/pc.	30	60	300
Advertising (6 classified ads @ $100 ea.)	600	600	600
Misc. (Supplies, etc.)	100	100	100
Total	$2,480	$4,960	$24,800

Income & Profit						
No. of pieces	500		1,000		5,000	
	Income	Profit	Income	Profit	Income	Profit
Sold @ $5	$2,500	$20	$5,000	$40	$25,000	$200
Sold @ $7	3,500	1,020	7,000	2,040	35,000	10,200
Sold @ $10	5,000	2,520	10,000	5,040	50,000	25,200

While the figures presented here are approximate, you can clearly see how widely profits can vary. Also, the costs reflect a worst-case scenario for start-up costs. As was mentioned previously, expenditures for materials and mailing might be delayed until orders come in, depending on how quickly you can assemble and prepare the orders for shipping.

Be careful in this area, however, because you never want to keep your customers waiting longer than is absolutely necessary. Many are the stories of small mail order businesses that have not made customer service their highest priority and have failed as a result.

If you are unable to fulfill an order for any reason, such as failure on the part of your supplier to meet demands, be sure to notify the customer in writing and keep them posted as to the status of their order.

Other Considerations

Another unique aspect of mail order merchandising is how perfectly it demonstrates the principles of free enterprise. While someone looking to build a new line of American automobiles, for example, risks becoming a target of the Detroit monopoly, anyone in mail order with a desirable product or service can successfully compete with the biggest of commercial firms.

As a matter of fact, when it comes to competition for mail order business, the more the better. The existence of other companies conditions the public to buy, and, more often than not, the small operator is selling something that is different than his or her competitors' product line. Think about it: What other business offers so many ready customers with so little competition?

An obvious question is what can you sell through mail order? A better question might be what *can't* you sell through mail order? The range of services and products available is staggering. In the course of an average day, you're probably at the receiving end of more mail order sales packages than you might think.

Between local advertising circulars, your favorite magazines, coupon packs (like Carol Wright), television, radio, and so on, you see *hundreds* of products being sold by mail every single day. From gummed return-address labels to exotic gourmet foods and everything in between, there is probably no other enterprise that offers such a wide range of goods as does mail order.

Top Sellers in Mail Order

As with any business, some products sell better than others. Here's a list of some of the more popular mail order goods:

♦ ***Books and newsletters.*** These items can make millions if properly marketed. The best type of books for mail order are motivational or how-to. Newsletters run the gamut from airplanes to the zodiac.

♦ ***Clothing.*** Because everyone needs clothes, this category is one of the biggest. The best sellers are handmade clothes, ethnic wardrobes, and lingerie, although just about any quality piece of clothing has a chance for success if properly advertised.

♦ ***Crafts items and services.*** Put your skills to work for you. Handmade toys, sweaters, pillows, decorating accessories, kits, patterns, supplies, and books never seem to go out of fashion.

♦ ***Food items.*** They do well, especially around the holidays. Home-cooked traditional items like fruitcakes or cookies in unusual containers are proven winners.

♦ ***Personalized products.*** Belt buckles, pens, stationery, children's items, handbags, and clothing are just a few of the offerings that do well.

♦ ***Vitamins and health products.*** These are very successful and popular with operators because they usually result in repeat orders. Your own label on vitamins or an exclusive on health items and clothing is a good bet.

If you think you'd rather sell a service, consider the skills you have to offer. What are your areas of special knowledge? Think about what information people seek: astrological, romance, facts, tips on everything from writing résumés to investing in the stock market. Let the market help you decide. Take a look at what is out there, get a sense for what is popular, then attempt to fill a gap. While services don't sell like products do, they're still a very viable aspect of mail order.

Each area has its advantages and disadvantages. Before you decide what your product or service will be, bear in mind that the ideal mail order product or service will appeal to men, women, and children of all ages, and will bring in repeat orders. Make the decision carefully; what you choose to sell is probably the most important decision you'll make in starting the business.

Ease of Start-up

One of mail order's most attractive aspects is the ease with which you can get a business started. How easy? Some of the most successful companies started as one-person ventures operating out of living rooms and garages. By starting small—that is, with one or two products—you can realistically get into the business for a few hundred dollars.

Of course, how quickly and easily your new effort gets off the ground will depend on what you're selling. Again, your biggest start-up headache may well be trying to decide what it is you want to sell. If all else fails, remember this: be a copycat. With mail order, it's smarter to sell a product that's already proven itself through the mail.

As with any business, the most important part of starting a mail order operation is planning. Most hassles you're likely to encounter in the beginning are nuts-and-bolts problems that can be avoided with careful planning: choosing a name, finding a printer, developing an effective advertising program, and so on.

Starting on a "Shoestring"

Start-up costs for a mail order business can vary, depending on

- ◆ How much time and money you want to commit
- ◆ How fast you want to grow
- ◆ What your product requires

Plenty of mail order firms have started on a shoestring budget of $100 or less. One such operator, three years into his part-time operation, has changed the business little since he started. He offers two instructional products and two low-priced booklets. His

focused product line and slow-growth approach allows him to keep overhead expenses down. His first costs were mostly for advertising and printing, and they remain about the same, with the added expense of shipping and handling.

Many experienced mail order business operators suggest that the neophyte start the business out small, as a sideline. Running a successful mail order operation requires a certain amount of knowledge that can only be learned by doing.

Here's a list of what you'll need to start on a shoestring budget:

1. Letterhead stationery
2. Address labels
3. Regular and business return envelopes
4. Pens
5. Writing or typing paper
6. A record book
7. Typewriter (you can rent at first)

It doesn't sound like much, but these are all the materials you'll need to get an ad written and printed and to prepare for shipping. Then, once the orders start coming in, you'll need to stock up on product and boxes or packaging to send items out to the customers.

The mail order industry is constantly buzzing with success stories about people who started small and saw significant returns their first time out. Such stories are true, but those successes can only happen when setup is approached with a good plan.

Qualifications

The mail order business is more accessible to the average person than, say, a retail store, regardless of his or her training or educational background.

There are no professional or academic degrees or certification of any kind required. And while there is no profile that can determine whether you're a good candidate for a mail order operation, if you possess certain business traits you'll probably do just fine. These traits include

- ◆ Organization for record-keeping and mailing schedules
- ◆ Motivation and perseverance because, as with any business, success doesn't happen overnight (although the right product and advertising campaign can result in a very fast profit)
- ◆ Willingness to work
- ◆ Flexibility and the ability to handle a variety of tasks, such as inventory control, packaging, advertising design, and placement
- ◆ Awareness of the mail order shopper's needs

If your goal is long-term involvement in the business, the time to begin developing success-oriented habits is from the very beginning. With that in mind, here's a checklist.

1. Find products that appeal to the consumer's needs.
2. Prepare creative advertising material that provides clear and simple details about your product(s) or service(s).
3. Develop an order system that is convenient and easy to use.
4. Maintain product quality at all times.
5. Ensure that "customer service" is the phrase of the day... every day.

Gardens were not made by singing "Oh, how beautiful"
and sitting in the shade.

Rudyard Kipling

Are you still not sure if mail order is the business for you? Let these words of assurance from the U.S. Department of Commerce bolster you: "In mail order work, anyone with imagination, determination, and a willingness to study and experiment should have very little difficulty getting started."

Notes

Key Points

Personal Thoughts

Additional Research

4

EQUIPMENT AND SUPPLIES

Office needs in this business are minimal, and paperwork can be taken care of very easily, especially if you maintain good records from the beginning. As the business grows, however, your administrative duties will increase: more jobs will be booked, calling for the preparation of contracts, lists, and employee information.

When your budget warrants it, start pricing equipment and supplies that you will eventually need to handle your administrative responsibilities efficiently.

There is no reason why you should pay high prices for office and working supplies. Check out office supply discount stores and wholesale catalogs and watch for sales. In all probability, everything needed to outfit an office can be purchased for at least 50 percent below standard retail prices.

General Office Equipment and Supplies

Desk and chair. You're going to be spending the majority of your time sitting at a desk doing paperwork, making telephone calls, and meeting clients. Check for something that not only gives you plenty of surface area to work on, but also provides a number of drawers to store frequently used items and papers.

It's extremely important that you invest in the right desk and chair. Not only will the wrong furniture give you backaches and neck aches, studies have proven that it can cause extreme fatigue and a decrease in overall productivity.

The chair you select should provide support for the base of the spine, a backrest no higher than your shoulder blades, and a seat that can be raised or lowered easily. A solid seat and rounded cushion to prevent the restriction of blood flow in the legs is recommended. The lumbar support and armrests should also be adjustable since everyone's body is proportioned differently. The best way to find the chair you need is to visit an office furniture store and try out several until you find one that feels comfortable.

You can save at least 30 percent by ordering the model you like through an office supply warehouse or by checking the classifieds and finding a firm that is going out of business or redecorating and selling off equipment and supplies.

Filing cabinet. An absolutely essential item is a filing cabinet to keep all of your papers in order. It is not enough to keep a ledger of income and expenses. You must also save all invoices, receipts, canceled checks, copies of orders, lists of customers' names, etc. If you employ help, you must keep payroll records as well.

Of course much of this information can be input and maintained directly on a computer if you have one, but there is still need for a simple filing system for "hard copy" and those paper odds and ends that must be saved for income tax purposes. All you need is a standard two- or four-drawer filing cabinet to begin with. Be sure, however, that you don't fall into the trap of buying your filing cabinet through a discount department store—typically these are substandard brands and frequently are not properly weighted. We've heard more than one story about drawers falling out or the whole cabinet falling over on some unsuspecting person.

Telephones. In a commercial location, getting a business telephone will be one of the first steps in setting up your business. If starting your business at home, you will likely be using your home telephone. However, plan to install a separate business line as soon as possible to maintain your professional image.

There is nothing more annoying to a client than being unable to get through because the personal line is tied up or having a child

answer a "business" phone, no matter how carefully they are trained to answer courteously. The advantage of a business line is that you can hook up an answering machine to intercept calls that come in after your established business hours.

Although it is still possible to rent telephones through certain telephone companies, the best bet is to buy your own. They are inexpensive, come in a variety of styles and colors, and are generally covered by a warranty.

Answering machines. Answering machines are an inexpensive way to ensure that your clients can leave a message when you're away from the office. Although there are still people who feel uncomfortable talking to a machine, anyone with an important message will overcome that discomfort, especially if your outgoing message is friendly. And with the popularity of answering machines increasing, the general public is becoming more used to them and less likely to hang up. In fact, some prospective clients may be highly annoyed if you do not have a machine to take their messages when you are out, since it is a waste of their time to keep calling you back in hopes of catching you in the office.

Machines are available in a wide range of prices. Top-of-the-line models may feature voice-activated messaging without time constraints, remote access codes that allow you to call in to your own line for messages when you're away, and a message counter featuring the time and date messages were left.

Adding machine or calculator. Calculators aren't expensive, especially the small, battery-operated kind, and they'll make your life much easier. Find one with at least an eight-figure display. Many computers include a built-in calculator and keypad. The advantage of an adding machine is that it provides a paper record of your figures, while a calculator provides only a temporary display.

Small card file box with alphabetical index. This will help you track inquiries and orders, and help build a mailing list. A 3 x 5 index-card box will do the job. A list of clients is essential, since much of your business will be from repeat customers. Give each customer his or her own card file with name, address, and telephone number at the top. The card will contain a record of

orders, charges, record of payment, etc. There is also computer software that will organize your client files in a similar way.

Additional Equipment Needs

As your business grows or in anticipation of success, some of the things you might want to add to your basic "office" materials include the following:

1. *Enhanced packaging equipment.* There are some things like special tape dispensers or package fill dispensers that, while generally expensive, will pay for themselves if your volume warrants their purchase.

2. *Postal meter.* You can hold off on this until you start getting over 100 orders a day. At that point, using a meter will be worthwhile.

3. *Inventory storage shelf.* Also for storage of forms, envelopes, ad materials, and so on. You can find a wide selection of shelving at any large home-improvement store.

4. *Postal scale.* Available at office supply stores. Make sure it can weigh in fractions of an ounce, up to at least one pound. Using the postal scale will help you keep postage costs down.

5. *Computer.* Certainly not a necessity, but it makes mail order much more efficient. It's possible to get a complete system—computer, monitor, and printer—for around $2,000; sometimes for less when the equipment is second-hand or a "clone" of more popular makes.

6. *Bookcase.* You might find yourself building a small library of reference materials, as well as holding on to various trade publications. Also, you will find that your printed matter (brochures, business cards, letterhead, etc.) takes up quite a bit of space. There might also be billing forms, order forms, and production supplies. Bookcases or shelving units will keep these items organized.

7. ***Rubber stamps.*** For the investment of a few dollars each, stamps save you a lot of writing and add a look to your work. Some of the stamps you'll find use for on a regular basis include

 ♦ Date stamp

 ♦ Company stamp with name, address, and phone number

 ♦ "Special Fourth Class Rate" for book mailing

 ♦ "First Class Mail"

 ♦ "Return Postage Guaranteed"

 ♦ "For Deposit Only–Account No.____"

 ♦ "Forwarding Postage Guaranteed"

 ♦ "Order Filled ____ Shipped ____ By ____"

 ♦ "Thanks for your order!"

 ♦ "Refund check"

 ♦ "Please pay–past due"

8. ***Copy machine.*** If you find yourself spending valuable time running back and forth to the nearest copy shop, it may be in your best interest to invest in a small home/office copier. However, weigh the benefits of a copy machine against the cost. If it's more cost-effective to go to your local copy shop, by all means do so.

The kinds of copiers available for low-volume use (considered to be no more than 500 copies per month) include thermal copiers, wet copiers, and plain-paper copiers, the latter being the most expensive. Options you'll want to consider include reduction and enlargement capabilities, collating, speed of printing, noise level of the copier, and the cost of supplies such as toner. Although you can find used copiers, you will often be buying someone else's problems. Copiers are notorious for requiring service, so the best bet is to buy or lease a new one from a company offering a solid service contract.

Miscellaneous Office Supplies

There's a range of office supplies you'll go through regularly. Find a local office supply store or a mail order office supplier (prices are often much better) for the following items:

- Address labels
- Billing forms
- Calendar, wall and/or desk
- Cellophane tape
- Computer paper and disks, if applicable
- Correction fluid
- Desk lamp
- Envelopes (manila)
- Erasers
- File folders and labels
- Job orders
- Letter opener
- Memo pads
- Paper clips
- Pencils and sharpener
- Pens, markers
- Postage stamps
- Printer ribbons/toner, if applicable

- Rubber bands
- Rubber cement
- Rubber fingertips
- Ruler
- Scissors
- Self-stick removable notes
- Shipping cartons
- Shipping labels (customized, if desired)
- Shipping tape
- Stamp moistener
- Stapler, staples, staple remover
- Stationery
- 3 x 5 inch cards and index tabs
- Utility knife and blades
- White glue
- Writing paper

All of these items are available from stationery or office supply stores or discount drugstores. You should be able to buy the supplies you need for under $150.

If buying in large quantities, consider ordering through catalog suppliers. Receipt of the merchandise may take longer, but the savings can be substantial.

Equipment Buying: New or Used?

You can buy new or used equipment from dealers and independent sellers. Or, if you don't mind rummaging through other people's lives, you can find incredible bargains on supplies and equipment at garage sales, swap meets, thrift shops run by charitable organizations, or auctions. Often, it is well worth the time involved because the savings can be significant.

Before investing money, do your homework. Talk with other business owners to find out which brand of equipment they use and why they prefer it over other choices on the market. This will help you make the best decision based on your needs and budget.

Also, talk with independent dealers who carry a broad line of similar types of equipment. They can give you insights on maintenance, longevity, service contracts, and prices.

They will also be able to tell you when to expect a drop in price for the item you are interested in, although you can count on seeing sales on major equipment such as postal meters and computers at store openings, during special sales, and during the first few months of the year, when manufacturers introduce their new models.

Cash or Credit?

Unless you are planning to pay cash for an equipment purchase, you will either make a down payment and set up a payment schedule with the dealer or take out a loan with the bank. You might be able to find a dealer who is willing to handle the financing at a lower rate than is available through a bank loan.

Although this method is a less effective way of establishing your credit, it will serve to get the business going. Another advantage is that if you should find yourself in a tight cash-flow situation at any time, a private dealer/lender with whom you have a personal relationship is much more likely to be flexible...without charging you a penalty for a late payment.

Buying Used Equipment

When buying used equipment from a dealer, the chances of it being in working condition are generally pretty good. Dealers have a reputation to uphold and will stand behind their merchandise, especially if they are firmly established in the community. There are, however, several ways you can scout around to ensure that the one you decide to work with is reputable.

◆ Find a store with membership in the local chamber of commerce. Although this is not an iron-clad guarantee, it does indicate the store owner's interest in following business standards established within the community.

◆ If the dealer also sells new equipment, it is highly likely that much of the used equipment has been traded in by people who are upgrading. You may be able to get an excellent deal on an item that has been carefully maintained by the former owner.

◆ If there is a service department on the premises, you can be assured that used equipment has been reconditioned before being put on sale. It also increases your chances of getting fast, inexpensive, and reliable service if needed at a later date.

◆ Used equipment dealers realize that it is not always easy to find a buyer and should be willing to work with you. Shopping around will give you an idea of average prices and will give you the information you need to negotiate. If the dealer won't work with you, keep looking.

◆ Know the terms of the warranty. Even used equipment should be covered for a short time for parts and labor, especially if it has been overhauled or reconditioned.

◆ Ask the dealer if he or she is willing to agree to offer a trade-in allowance on the item you are buying when you decide to upgrade. Of course, there will be stipulations based on wear and tear and time; however, the dealer should be willing to consider it.

♦ Contact your local Better Business Bureau to see if any complaints have been made about the dealer.

Buyer Beware

There are other ways to find and buy used equipment, but it falls into the realm of "buyer beware." If you choose to deal with private parties through the classified ads or with auctioneers selling off the inventory of a bankrupt business, you must be willing to take a chance. Although the prices will be easy on your budget, the cost of repairing a malfunctioning machine could result in a long-term drain on your profits.

This is not to say that there aren't good opportunities out there. The secret is to know what you are looking for and to have a good idea of how it should work. Do your research by visiting with reliable used-equipment dealers before you start looking.

Ask a private party how long they have owned the equipment, why it is being sold, and if there are any repair bills that you can look at. Trust your intuition in this kind of situation; if the party seems truly interested in providing you with as much information as possible, chances are the equipment is as claimed. If you're told it needs a new part, for example, find out what the replacement part costs and ask if that amount could be deducted from the selling price.

Ask a private party how long they have owned the equipment, why it is being sold, and if there are any repair bills that you can look at.

When you go to see the equipment, make sure it runs. Test it out, if possible, and measure it to make sure it will fit into the space you have available. Also, see whether you can move it yourself or will have to arrange transportation.

Before buying the equipment try to find out if there is a servicing outlet nearby or if you must send away for parts, which

can be time-consuming and costly, especially when it comes to older models.

Occasionally you will run across an individual who is making payments on a piece of equipment still under warranty. This can be a great deal for you since he or she will probably accept a small amount of cash and let you take over the payments. Be sure to transfer ownership in writing to prevent complications if you need service under the warranty.

Auctions

Auctions are an excellent way to get equipment and supplies at good prices. Watch the business and classified sections of the newspaper for ads about upcoming auctions. The ad will include dates, the reason for the auction (liquidation or bankruptcy), location, time, and a partial list of items. In most cases there will be a preview, enabling potential buyers to view the merchandise before the bidding begins. Take advantage of the preview to inspect and select the equipment you want to bid on. A fee will be required for a bidder registration number, which is held up when you make a bid so the auctioneer's spotters know who has purchased a particular item.

There are two rules to remember at auctions:

1. Cash or a personal check for the full purchase amount must be paid on the day of the auction.

2. Don't move your hands or make significant gestures during bidding or you might find that you have purchased something you didn't want.

Leasing Equipment

Leasing is defined as a long-term agreement between two parties for the use of a specific item. The person who leases is known as the lessee, while the owner of the item is referred to as the lessor.

Despite the fact that you do not own the equipment when you lease, and so cannot take advantage of depreciation on it for tax purposes, there are still many benefits for the beginning business owner who leases.

Leasing lets you try out a piece of equipment for a given period of time to determine if it is the best product for your needs. Although you are locked in to the terms of the lease, most lessors are flexible.

Know What You Need

Of course, the best way to enter into a lease is to be absolutely clear about what you expect the equipment to do for you. The service representative from the leasing company is well-versed in tailoring equipment to the customer, so do not hesitate to ask questions about capabilities.

Most lessors offer good maintenance contracts, as they want to protect their equipment. Check to see what parts and/or labor are covered before signing the lease. The lessor should also be willing to provide technical advice at no charge, may be willing to offer installation and setup of the equipment, and may also provide training, if required.

Payments can be arranged to fit your budgetary needs on a monthly, semiannual, or annual basis. This gives you the freedom to schedule payments for peak cash-flow periods. You can also negotiate the rates and length of the lease to keep monthly operating expenses at a minimum.

Conditional Sales Agreement

Under the provisions of a conditional sales agreement, you become the owner of the leased goods from the agreement date. At the end of the lease period, you are required to purchase the item for a preestablished price. This is often referred to as a balloon payment and should be agreed upon by you and the lessor prior to your signing the lease.

The conditional sales agreement, unlike most other leasing contracts, gives you the tax advantage of claiming depreciation on equipment. Depreciation refers to the decrease in the value of an asset because of wear and tear over a period of time.

You are entitled to deduct depreciation from your income tax based on the value when new, the estimated life of the item, and the value at the end of that estimated life. It is best to work with your accountant on determining depreciation of fixed assets.

There is seldom a down payment, other than the first month's lease amount, required on a leased item, since leasing is generally 100 percent financed for the terms of the agreement. This frees your start-up or working capital for other uses.

True Lease Agreements

You can write off lease payments on your income tax, but only if you have a true lease contract. Under a true lease, the lessor owns the equipment at all times during the contract period. If you decided, at the end of the lease, that you wanted to buy the equipment, you would have to pay whatever purchase price was decided by the lessor.

Financial Lease

The financial lease covers a period that does not extend beyond the estimated life of the equipment. Payments must be made as stipulated on the date due and made consistently to the end of the lease. It usually puts the responsibility and cost of maintenance on the lessee.

Operating Lease

The operating lease generally requires the lessor to handle maintenance of the equipment. It offers the option of canceling the lease, but only if a cancellation clause has been included at the negotiating stage.

The most important aspects of leasing are the terms outlined in the formal lease. Have the lessor draw up a proposal for you, based on everything you have discussed in an initial meeting. If you have any trouble understanding the terms of the proposal, have your accountant review it with you. In fact, it is a definite advantage to have the final lease agreement checked by your attorney or accountant before you sign it.

Your Lease Agreement

Your lease agreement should include

♦ The length of the contract in months or years

♦ The rate you are to be charged, which is usually a percentage of the total purchase price computed on a monthly rate

♦ Your payment schedule

♦ A purchase option, if applicable, at the end of the lease

♦ A renewal option, if applicable, which allows you to carry the lease over for an additional period of time

♦ A cancellation agreement in the event you want or need to cancel the lease

♦ Maintenance stipulations (who pays for parts and labor)

♦ Substitution options if updated equipment is introduced and you want to take advantage of improvements

♦ Any provisions particular to the lease, including tax allowances for depreciation, insurance liability in case of loss or damage, and your responsibilities in reporting a move or other major change

Whether you decide to borrow, buy new equipment, find good used equipment, or lease, be sure to get exactly what you need to keep costs to a minimum. This is especially important during the early stages of your business when cash is bound to be tight. You can always upgrade or add to your equipment inventory as profits increase.

Start-up Costs

(Based on average investment using home as office)

Basic office needs (desk, filing cabinet, etc.)	$1,000.00
Office supplies	150.00
Licenses, permits, fictitious name statement	100.00
Initial inventory of products	250.00
Utilities and telephone deposits	150.00
Legal and accounting start-up consultation	200.00
Insurance (3 months)	250.00
Advertising & promotion	3,000.00
Total	**$5,100.00**

For higher investment start-up with more than one product, add:

Rent (first and last month) for warehouse/office	$2,500.00
Leasehold improvements	1,500.00
Color catalog of products (design & printing)	15,000.00
Inventory of products	5,000.00
Total	**$29,100.00**

Notes

Key Points

Personal Thoughts

Additional Research

5

START-UP BASICS

Having decided that you are ready and able to accept the challenge of starting your own business, it is necessary to take a look at your overall financial picture. Even if you have a healthy savings account, or feel you can start your business with a minimal capital investment, diagnosing your personal financial situation will help you determine ongoing expenses.

The easiest way to estimate exactly how much money you will need to get your business started and to cover expenses, including personal living expenses for the first six months, is to prepare a *Cash Flow Statement* and a *Projected Expense Statement*. Samples are provided in this chapter.

Preparing the Projected Expense Statement will give you a fairly accurate picture of what it will cost to open the doors and will indicate how much income you must generate to realize a profit. Another advantage of creating these charts early in the game is that two of the required documents will already be prepared when you want to explore funding options, then you will only need to update them.

The first step in examining your financial situation is to ask yourself the following questions:

1. Do I generally pay my bills on time or do I wait until my creditors start sending me collection notices?
2. Have I regularly reconciled my bank statement so I know how much money I have in my checking account at any given time?
3. Is my philosophy "If I've got it, I spend it" or do I carefully plan how I am going to use my income?
4. Have I ever developed a personal budget so I know how much money is coming in, how much is going out, and what I have left over?

These are important aspects of your financial personality that will be helpful to understand when running your business. As your business and subsequent involvement with financial matters grow, it will be vital that you have a handle on your philosophy about money. And there is no time like in the beginning, when your business concept is being formed, to start learning.

The Cash Flow Statement

Use the Cash Flow Statement at the end of this chapter to determine your personal living expenses for the past three to six months to help you gauge what you will need to survive during the early stages of your business.

The easiest way to complete the statement is to use your checkbook register or sales receipts as research tools. If your expenses are relatively consistent from month to month, you should be able to get an overview by analyzing one month. A more accurate picture will emerge if you break down income and expense for three to six months to account for periodic payments, such as taxes, insurance, and seasonal spending.

Using the samples provided, fill in the amounts in each category from your checkbook register or receipts. Use a separate sheet for every month that you are analyzing. For miscellaneous spending, a standard calculation is 5 percent of monthly income.

Add up each month's expenses, total them all, and then divide that figure by the number of months you are analyzing. This will give you an average monthly expense figure.

Follow the same procedure for income. You can then subtract your expenses from your income to see where you stand. If you have computed your figures accurately, you might run across a few surprises. It isn't unusual to discover that we spend more money than we realize, often on unnecessary purchases. You may be able to see some areas where you can cut back.

The main points, however, are that you now know

1. How much or whether you can afford to invest your own money in your new business

2. What it costs for you to live comfortably, which will help you set income goals for the business

A six-month cost projection will be a good indicator not only of expenses near-term, but the kinds of profits you can expect as the business gets underway.

Start-up Costs

Every business owner has specific standards about how he or she wants to run the operation. One person may feel perfectly comfortable waiting to order business cards until there is a profit. Another wouldn't dream of opening the doors without cards, brochures, and letterhead already printed.

You will have your own ideas about what you need before opening your business. Then you must find out what it will cost and, if at all possible, prepare the *Start-up Costs Worksheet* at the end of this chapter.

It is also advisable to figure how much it will cost to run the business for three to six months, using the sample Projected Expense Statement. A six-month projection should give you the opportunity to determine your profits down the line.

Preparing the Start-up Costs Worksheet and Projected Expense Statement involves conducting some research. For example, to estimate the cost of business cards or letterhead stationery, contact several printers or copy shops in your area and obtain

quotes. Call the local newspaper for prices on different types of ads, including display and classified.

An insurance agent will be able to give you an estimate on liability coverage. Check with the telephone company for information and rates on installing a phone line.

You can also start to shop around to find the best prices on office supplies, equipment, and materials needed to conduct business.

After you have completed your research, incorporate the information on the blank charts. Obviously, some of your figures, such as those for telephone expenses, will be guesstimated. However, the final figure will give you a good idea of start-up and operational costs for the first six months.

Utilizing the same theory, you can develop a *Projected Income Statement* (worksheet not provided), drawing from industry figures available through your trade association or other research sources. This would include all income realized from cash sales, collection on outstanding invoices, credit card sales, and miscellaneous income. By subtracting your total expenses from total income, you will get a clear picture of projected profit or loss.

All of these statements will be requested by loan officers, venture capitalists, and the Small Business Administration if and when you apply for a loan. This kind of paperwork is required to ensure that you have basic business knowledge, a commendable track record, and are serious about your venture. You will also be required to fill out a personal financial statement, available through the lending institution, especially if you are the sole owner or a general partner in the business.

Cash Flow Statement
Month of _____

Income		Expenses	
Wages	$_____	Rent or mortgage	$_____
Miscellaneous	$_____	Auto loan	$_____
		Gas & auto repairs	$_____
TOTAL	$_____	Auto insurance	$_____
		Life insurance	$_____
		Medical insurance	$_____
Savings	$_____	Homeowner's insurance	$_____
		Taxes	$_____
Credit Line	$_____	Loan payments	$_____
		Food: At home	$_____
		Food: Dining out	$_____
Home Equity	$_____	Telephone	$_____
		Utilities	$_____
		Household repairs, etc.	$_____
		Medical bills	$_____
		Credit card payments	$_____
		Interest expense	$_____
		Clothing/dry cleaning	$_____
		Travel	$_____
		Miscellaneous	$_____
		Savings	$_____
		TOTAL	$_____

Start-up Costs Worksheet

Furniture: Purchase price $_____

 Down payment required $_____

Fixtures: Purchase price _____

 Down payment required _____

Equipment: Purchase price _____

 Down payment required _____

Installation and delivery costs _____

Decorating & leasehold improvements _____

Deposits: Utilities and rent _____

Fees: Legal, accounting, consulting, etc. _____

Licenses & permits _____

Starting inventory _____

Supplies _____

Printing _____

Initial advertising & promotion _____

Miscellaneous _____

Total Start-up Expense $_____

Less Available Start-up Capital $_____

Total Amount Needed $_____

Projected Expense Statement

Months	1st	2nd	3rd	4th	5th	6th
Rent						
Utilities						
Telephone						
Insurance						
Professional services						
Taxes & licenses						
Advertising						
Office supplies						
Office equipment						
Inventory						
Business auto expense						
Travel expense						
Entertainment						
Dues & subscriptions						
Salaries						
Owner's draw						
Loan payments						
Interest payments						
Miscellaneous						
TOTALS						

6

POTENTIAL CLIENTS

The mail order business is in full swing and is expected to grow steadily over the next decade. The increased purchase of goods and services by mail is primarily based on recent societal changes, including a greater number of professionals in the workplace, higher incomes, and the fact that taking time out to physically go shopping after a busy workday is something that seven out of ten adults just can't do. So these days, just about everyone buys items through the mail at one time or another, meaning that your market could be considered to be unlimited. Of course, mail order, like any business, has its trends.

It was once the shopping salvation for people who lived in rural areas, away from stores or a selection of products. Now the majority of mail order shoppers are city dwellers. More discretionary income, but less time to spend it, has made mail order a boon for a large portion of the population.

Step into the psyche of the average customer:

It's the end of a busy day—the dinner dishes are done, the children are tucked into bed, and the house is quiet. Time to sit back after having fought traffic, the job, and piles of paperwork. What better way to spend an evening than with

a freshly brewed cup of coffee, a pen, and a few mail order
catalogs...take care of some shopping and do a little wishing?

This is a common scenario, and may well be one you have
personally experienced. Last year more than 30 percent of the
American population willingly paid for the convenience of shop-
ping from their living room couch. (Many claim they shop by mail
for the thrill of receiving the packages... it's like Christmas every
time a package arrives!)

Your customers are easy to identify. They're probably a lot
like you, with the same basic interest in finding good values that
will, in some small way, make their lives a little more enjoyable.
With that in mind, let's say that your customers are interested in
better health, more money, popularity, comfort, leisure, accom-
plishment, appearance, security, praise, advancement, more fun,
pride, "keeping up with the Joneses," creativity, efficiency, influ-
ence, self-improvement, being "in," humor, drama, food and drink,
movies, television, sports, watching their kids grow... the list
could fill this book.

Where do your customers live? Everywhere. From lifelong
residents of Smalltown, U.S.A., to people living overseas, mail
order serves the most far-flung client base of any business on
earth. That's part of the beauty of mail order. You can serve
someone on a Navy base in Rota, Spain, just as efficiently as a
customer a few miles down the road.

Who are your customers? Anyone with a mailbox. And
everyone has a mailbox. All you have to do is get their attention,
which you do by advertising, covered in Chapter 20.

Potential Customers

Acquaintances and Service Providers

Business Contacts

Friends and Relatives

7

A MARKETING OVERVIEW

Now that you have selected the kind of business you want to own, it is important to explore the need for it. A process known as *marketing research* will provide you with the information you need to develop your mail order service, plan methods of distribution or promotion, and set prices that are tailored to the audience you hope to attract.

In addition, your marketing research will provide you with information that will help when you make decisions about a location, hours of operation, the specific types of services and/or products to sell, and how to gear your advertising.

Identifying Your Market

The process of identifying your audience may seem to be an extremely complex process; however, you can develop a perfectly workable and valuable marketing report by using the following guidelines and adapting them to your particular situation. Basically, there are five factors used to target the market.

Five Factors Used to Target Your Market

1. Population
2. Income
3. Competition
4. Product or service market match
5. Desire

1. ***Population.*** The number of households in the region you are considering for your business is crucial, as you must have a sufficient population base to produce the sales you need to generate a profit. Equally important is the circulation and age range of readers of the publications where you will be placing your advertising for specific products. If, for example, you are planning to sell products for infants, a publication whose readership is largely of retirement age would be inappropriate. It would, however, work in your favor if you were promoting health products or gift items.

2. ***Income.*** Your potential customers must have the income to purchase goods and services. Consumers in the thirty-five to sixty-five age group generally have considerable income to spend on household items, personal grooming, and sporting goods. This is not to discount the over-sixty-five age group, a large and growing segment of the nation's population which, depending on the region, has adequate discretionary income (money after taxes and necessities) to spend, or the eighteen to thirty-five age group, which is a desirable market for clothing, personal, and recreational items.

3. ***Competition.*** Competition shouldn't be a negative factor. Rather, it should spur you on to stretch your creativity by creating something brand new or creating a similar product or service that is superior to those being offered by the competition—through quality, selection, or price.

4. ***Product or service market match.*** Basically, this means that you must be able to attract those consumers whom you have the resources to serve. For example, if your idea of the perfect business involves national distribution of your patented weight-training equipment, you must reach an audience that is receptive and interested in bodybuilding through a carefully designed advertising campaign, and have the financing available to supply and ship the product.

5. ***Desire.*** Your objective is to match your product or service to the needs and desires of a particular group of consumers who will be responsive. It is often difficult to figure out exactly what your target market wants. However, through observation of what the competition is doing, it should be possible to recognize a need.

Market Research Techniques

Large corporations often have in-house marketing staffs who conduct extensive research on a continuing basis to ensure that the products or services being offered are in line with the marketplace. Obviously, this is an expensive and time-consuming process; one that you undoubtedly want to avoid.

Through several easy and inexpensive methods, you can find out everything you want to know about your potential market. But first you need to determine exactly what information you need. It might be population or economic trends, the number of new homes built locally within the last five years, or how many people are active in a particular hobby.

The greater the difficulty, the more glory there is in surmounting it. Skillful pilots gain their reputations from storms and tempests.

Anonymous

The nearest Census Bureau office and your local chamber of commerce are consistently good sources for regional statistics. The reference librarian at the public library can steer you toward other data that will give you the specifics you seek.

The Small Business Administration (SBA) compiles extensive marketing information, in addition to material on operating procedures for specific types of businesses.

Check the *Encyclopedia of Associations* at the library to find the name and address of the advisory board for the mail order industry. Trade boards can provide associates with marketing statistics, management tips, and a wealth of valuable information. Often it only takes a phone call to get more details than you could ever use.

Another excellent source of information on population, income, and sales figures is the annual survey of buying power published by *Sales and Marketing Management Magazine,* which breaks the information down by county and cities in the United States and should be available through the library.

Media Kits and Personal Contact

The advertising departments of local magazines and newspapers undoubtedly have a "media kit" available for potential advertisers, which they will gladly send you upon request. These packets contain a breakdown of their advertising rates and specifications, a description of why advertising with them is to your benefit and, most important, a profile of their readership. A friendly conversation with one of their salespeople should give you a wealth of data.

The merchants from whom you will be buying supplies, equipment, and products are another excellent source. They can give you a good rundown on trends, as well as an overview of current sales figures for their products. Since they are hoping you will eventually use them as a supplier for your business, they will be more than happy to give you free information.

It is, of course, often possible to gauge what the competition is doing and to glean information from them. There are two approaches when talking to people who are soon to be in direct competition. One is to be up-front and honest about your business plans and appeal to their sense of "industry spirit."

Surprisingly, you will find the direct approach works in the majority of cases as most people are genuinely interested in and supportive of others trying to make it in their field. It is better for everyone if "industry" standards are maintained and competitors have a healthy rapport. And, except in extreme situations such as a very small community, there is generally enough business to go around. It shouldn't be difficult to capture your share of the market, especially if you can develop something unique to attract them.

On the other hand, if competitors are less than receptive, it may be necessary to do some detective work to get the information you want.

Focus Groups

If you really want to go into depth with your marketing study, you might consider gathering together a group of people (family members, a social or church group, or friends) for a focus session to determine if your product or service will match the needs of the prospective audience. This involves presenting your proposed business idea, with product samples if applicable, and creating a questionnaire that calls for specific answers from the group members.

The greatest thing in the world is not so much where we stand as in what direction we are moving.

Oliver Wendell Holmes

This method is often used by companies when they are testing new products and, in fact, there are private companies that do nothing but put focus groups together and set up testing sites in stores, shopping malls, and street corners to obtain spontaneous and objective input from potential consumers.

The questions you would want to include on your questionnaire would cover such aspects as how often members of the focus group have used a similar service or product in the past, what they

liked about it, what they found to be unsatisfactory, how they feel it could have been improved, whether they would be willing to try another, and vital statistics such as their age, income, and any specifics that relate to your proposed business.

With your mail order business, the questions might include a breakdown of the top three reasons people in your focus group ordered from a particular company, what they liked and disliked about the way their order was handled, and how they originally found out about the product or mail order house. This kind of information will give you an immediate edge on the competition when you are ready to start advertising.

Analyzing Your Research

The bottom line in conducting your research is that you want to zero in on information that provides insights on the potential for your business idea before you invest time, money, and energy in setting it up.

If, for example, you were considering starting your business in a small community, and your focus group information indicated that only 10 percent of the local residents would consider using your service or product, you would definitely want to reconsider the validity of your concept or figure ways to promote it on a broader scale.

On the other hand, if your marketing research pointed out that 90 percent of the population thought it was a great idea and that 50 percent would have an immediate need for it, the potential for your business would be much greater, and proceeding with the idea would probably guarantee a profitable venture.

Buy an inexpensive notebook to help you keep track of your marketing data. Use a separate page for each category you are researching. The notebook will serve as your personal, ongoing market study to be reviewed and amended as your business grows and the audience you are serving changes.

Plan to update your information as new studies are published (generally an annual event), indicating changes in population, economy, or buying and spending trends. Most newspapers publish synopses of local, state, and federal studies of this nature, so maintain your notebook as appropriate. You should also reserve

several pages to record comments and suggestions from customers once your business is established, which will help you personalize the service to the market and keep you a step ahead of the competition.

Spend as much time as needed to feel comfortable about your marketing project. The important point is that the results of your research are comprehensive enough to provide you with concrete information on who your potential customers are and how you can best reach them.

Review

I have completed my entrepreneurial profile to determine my strengths and weaknesses. _____

My friends and family have given me additional input based on the profile. _____

I am aware of the advantages and disadvantages of going into business for myself. _____

Time is not a problem; I can easily devote the time I'll need to build my business. _____

The important people in my life are supportive of my decision. _____

I have analyzed my cash flow to ensure that I can support myself and my family for at least six months or until the business is solvent. _____

I feel confident about my future as a business owner at this point. _____

I know what people want as far as my business is concerned. _____

I have conducted informal studies to determine my potential customers and understand their needs. _____

I have analyzed the competition, know what they offer, and have a general idea about their success ratio. _____

I have done my marketing research and know how to get in touch with the audience I want to reach. _____

I have contacted the trade association for my industry and have accumulated facts and figures regarding the pros and cons of starting my own business. _____

I am confident that my product or service is marketable. _____

Notes

Target Audience

Publications to Advertise In

Additional Research Information

8

Location: Commercial Versus Home-Based

The Home Office

In this business, it doesn't matter where you locate the business since you will be relying on advertising in regional or national publications to promote and sell your products or services. The only requirement is proximity to a post office or a packaging and shipping facility for receiving and fulfilling orders.

If you are planning on setting up the operation in your home, your space requirements are essentially taken care of. Unless your business grows so large that you need an office, you'll do fine with a corner of the living room or even a corner of the kitchen table for some time. This greatly reduces start-up costs normally required for renting an office and outfitting it.

Of course, no matter where you set up the business, you should be as kind to yourself as possible. You'll be spending a lot of time sitting and stuffing envelopes, so allow yourself a certain level of comfort when you choose a work space. If your home has a den or workshop, set up in one of those rooms. Maybe your garage provides a perfect spot and enough room to meet your needs.

Depending on the products you sell, your home business will either be barely noticeable or will become so obtrusive that mates and children will scream. Anticipate your working and storage needs based on your product. How big is the item itself? Thousands of earrings, especially unassembled ones, won't take up much space when kept in boxes. Packing materials will add to the space needs, but not much if your product is small.

On the other hand, if your product is, say, a booklet, you'll need an appreciable amount of wall space for boxes of printed material. The larger the product and its associated shipping materials, the more space you'll need. Plan ahead as much as possible.

The way you lay out your work space should be based on the type of work you'll be doing. The general business of mail order will have you stuffing envelopes and doing paperwork. No problem, since just about any flat surface will suffice—though, again, you want to make sure you're comfortable.

But what about your product? Is there some sort of assembly work that requires a large workbench? Do you need room to wrap and box items?

An ideal workplace will allow you to integrate all aspects of your mail order operation without having to move from room to room around the house. As your business grows, you'll want to produce as much volume as efficiently as you can. To do that, you need a comfortable, logically laid out work space that won't have you knocking your elbows against the walls or disrupting the family routine.

Fulfillment

You can keep start-up costs low by signing on with a fulfillment center that will handle all the shipping and much of the paperwork. The center gets a percentage of every sale to process mail or telephone orders (if you have an 800 number), track inventory, and generate packaging and shipping.

Setting Up Your Business at Home

There is a lot of appeal in operating your business from home. Thousands of successful businesses have been started in a basement, a spare room, or on the kitchen table. It's true that Henry Ford founded the Ford Motor Company in his garage and Jean Nidetch started Weight Watchers in her living room as a support group for friends who wanted to lose extra pounds. Both of these businesses, and many more like them, became successful multimillion-dollar corporations despite humble beginnings.

The Small Business Administration estimates that there are close to twenty million home-based businesses in the United States today and, of these, more than 30 percent are owned and operated by women.

Starting a home-based business has provided an opportunity for many people who might otherwise never have the chance to become business owners. Women, especially, have discovered that they can build a profitable, satisfying business at home while still being available for their families.

For others, a home-based business is the ticket out of the world of the urban commuter. In fact, a home-based business is the perfect way to try something new to see how it works while still working another job to pay the bills. Once the business has proven itself and is realizing a profit, you can leave the job to devote all your time to your new venture.

Couples often find that investing time and energy in building a business together at home develops stronger relationships in addition to increasing joint income. For the retired and for those with minor physical disabilities, it is a path to staying involved, exploring self-sufficiency, and guaranteeing that there can be a profitable future.

Start-ups Never Change

As with any new business, whether located at home or in a commercial location, it is important to follow the basic guidelines for start-up, including conducting a market survey, drawing up a business plan, setting goals, reviewing capital needs and projected

income, developing an advertising campaign, and establishing a professional image.

Advantages of a Home-Based Business

◆ Ability to start your business immediately

◆ Minimal start-up capital needed

◆ No rent or excessive setup charges for utilities

◆ Comfortable working conditions

◆ Reduced wardrobe expenses

◆ No commuting

◆ Tax benefits

◆ Elimination of office politics

◆ Flexibility and independence

◆ Full utilization and recognition of skills

◆ Low risk for trial and error

Many businesses, especially in the areas of service and mail order, can easily be set up in the home, offering a number of advantages for the beginning business owner. Setting up your business at home automatically eliminates up to 75 percent of the start-up costs and responsibilities required for an office or storefront operation. You are, in your home, already making rent or mortgage payments and paying for your own telephone service, insurance, and utilities. (In many instances, a commercial location will require $10,000 just to open the doors with basic leasehold improvements and/or equipment.) In addition, valuable time and energy are saved because you don't have to scout for the location, have utilities installed, and decorate the premises.

Getting Your Feet Wet

A home-based business gives you the opportunity to test the waters with a minimum of risk. This is especially beneficial to first-time entrepreneurs, who may prefer to learn and grow with the business in the comfort of home without the pressures that operating out of a commercial location often bring.

As a hedge against inflation, the home-based business is a natural. In addition to low start-up, tax deductions for use of a home office and business expenses provide relief from a seemingly endless outflow of cash spent on mortgage or rent payments. You must, however, be aware of the tax laws, which allow deductions only for that part of the home "used exclusively and regularly" for business and limited to a modified net income of the business.

After the business is running smoothly, you will find that the potential to earn money is greater because of reduced overhead. Your production will increase because you have more control over your schedule and fewer of the typical interruptions that arise in a commercial setting. Of course, as with any business arrangement, there are also disadvantages to setting up your business in your home. By recognizing them, however, it is possible to address and minimize the problems before they come up.

Disadvantages of a Home-Based Business

♦ Success is based 100 percent on your efforts

♦ Difficult to establish solid work habits

♦ Difficult to determine competitive rates

♦ Limited support system

♦ Isolation

♦ Limited work space

♦ Disruption of personal life

♦ Clients are uncomfortable coming to your home

♦ Zoning restrictions

Getting to Work

One of the biggest problems faced by home-based entrepreneurs is being able to establish a productive work schedule. There are different types of interruptions that come up in a home environment, including visits from friends and neighbors, household chores that need to be done, the temptation of television and the daily paper when there is work to be produced, and the fact that there is no one around to spur you on.

A helpful suggestion for getting down to work is to dress in the morning as if you were going out to a regular job. This alone will help you set your priorities for the day.

The best solution, however, is to establish regular working hours at the outset (although you do have the flexibility as a home-based business owner to arrange your schedule around the times you know you are the most productive). If friends want to visit, politely explain to them that you are operating a business that requires your full concentration and arrange a suitable time to get together according to your schedule.

It is also important, if you have family, that they are supportive and willing to arrange their lives as much as possible around your schedule. This can be dealt with through frequent family discussions about what you are doing and how the business operates.

Another difficult area is learning to separate business and pleasure. A home-based business often makes it very easy to work day and night on a project. Again, it is important to allot time for personal activities. The point to remember is that the work will get done much more efficiently if you are relaxed and rested.

It is also a good idea to have the business set up in a separate room or area that can be shut off from your personal living space after working hours. This will more easily enable you to separate work from leisure time.

Home-based business owners often experience feelings of isolation from those in their industry. One way to eliminate this is to join local groups, such as the chamber of commerce and networking groups, and to attend the meetings. Check to see how many members are entrepreneurs, which will give you a built-in support system. By making yourself available to serve on commit-

tees, you'll be able to reach into the community and publicize your business for the cost of your involvement.

Reviewing Local Laws

Before getting started, it is important to check that zoning ordinances in your area will allow you to use your home for business purposes. Since zoning ordinances vary from city to city and county to county, it is necessary to contact the planning department of your regional government offices or talk with your attorney to find out what is allowed, based on the type of business, the area to be used within your home, noise control, tax regulations, business signs, and other aspects, as well as if you need a special permit or license to operate.

If you are expecting clients to visit your home for business, it is best to have a separate room set up as an office so that when they do come to discuss your product or service, they won't feel as if they are intruding on a family. If, however, an office is out of the question, make sure you arrange meetings during times when the family is away from home to ensure that there will be no interruptions.

Another option is to go to the client's location when you must have meetings or to offer pickup and delivery service, if applicable. Depending on the business, however, and the quality of your work, client discomfort shouldn't be a major problem, according to a number of home-based business owners we have interviewed.

The number of home-based businesses has increased dramatically over the past few years. The bottom line, as far as the customer is concerned, is—and will always be—reliable service and high-quality products and the knowledge they are dealing with a professional.

God gives every bird its food, but He does not throw it in the nest.

J.G. Holland

The benefits of a home-based business to the beginning entrepreneur can mean the difference between working for someone else or turning a dream into reality. The key elements, as with any business, are motivation, a needed product or service, careful planning, and the desire to succeed. Just knowing that the expenses of establishing a business in a commercial location are alleviated by setting up a home-based enterprise is enough to push you forward to success, one small step after another.

Utilities and Phone

The home-based business has an additional advantage: Your phone line and utilities are already in place. Any additional equipment is easy to obtain from your utility carriers because you already have an established payment history.

Single-line telephone systems are adequate for most small businesses, but when your business outgrows a single-line system, you'll need a multiline system enabling you to accept several calls simultaneously and switch between lines.

Regardless of whether you need a single line or a multiline telephone system, some options are now available when choosing equipment.

Programmable memory allows automatic storage and instant dialing of phone numbers by pressing a button or entering a code.

Automatic redial reconnects the last number dialed, in some cases redialing at specific intervals until the call goes through.

Speed dialing allows you to quickly access frequently dialed numbers by using a one- to four-digit code.

Call waiting is especially useful for businesses with single lines, allowing you to take incoming calls while putting the original caller on hold.

Conference calling is often a related feature of call waiting, allowing you to simultaneously speak with two or more parties at different locations.

Call forwarding routes incoming calls to a preprogrammed phone number at another location.

Cordless phones are especially useful for the home business, allowing you to make or accept calls from any location in the

house. Because cordless phones vary in quality, it's strongly recommended that you research the market thoroughly before buying.

Speaker phones allow you to carry on conversations without the constraint of holding a receiver. One of the main benefits is that you can accomplish other tasks while waiting on hold. They're also useful for note taking and similar chores during business conversations.

Voice mail is a combination answering, routing, and messaging system that can help cut front-office payroll costs (if you have a staff) while maximizing efficiency. Customers dialing a voice-mail number are greeted by a recorded message and given a menu of options: direct-dialing employees in other departments, leaving messages for one or more individuals, receiving additional recorded information, and using the voice-mail system with a rotary-dial phone.

The cost of voice mail has been scaled down dramatically in recent years and is now available for small or even one-person businesses, presenting a first-class image while actually saving you money (not only in payroll costs but in avoiding potential lost revenues from unanswered or misdirected calls).

Long-Distance Carriers

Whether you're a one-person, home-based operation or an expanding business in a commercial location, long-distance service is, of course, essential.

The host of carriers competing for your long-distance dollar, their conflicting claims, and a wide range of services can bewilder the small business owner trying to make a choice.

When deciding which carrier to use for your business, consider the following:

♦ Areas of the country and the world that you will most frequently be calling

♦ Monthly amount you anticipate spending on long-distance calls

♦ Time of day you'll be making most of your calls

♦ Seasonal calling patterns

♦ Whether you'll be dealing only with clients statewide (a regional WATS line would be a cost-effective choice)

In addition, read the various carriers' promotional information carefully. Does the carrier you're considering charge start-up or installation fees or a flat monthly fee? If the latter, will you meet the carrier's minimum usage requirements and are the services offered worth the monthly charge?

Other factors to consider include available volume discounts based on usage and dedicated lines giving you exclusive access to a telecommunications network.

800 Numbers

Businesses that market products and services regionally or nationally have found the 800 number to be one of their most effective marketing tools. Customers who might not otherwise pay for a long-distance call now pick up the phone without hesitation—and frequently wind up requesting further information about services or making hefty credit card purchases.

Though 800 numbers can pay for themselves thousands of times over, the installation fees, service charges, and usage fees can be expensive. Consider carefully whether the potential costs outweigh the benefits. An alternative is the localized 800 number, available for small, highly targeted geographic areas. Consult your phone company's service representative for further information.

Mail Order Businesses

If most of your business is conducted through the mail or delivery services, location selection can be based on rent, the amount of space needed, and the convenience to you. When choosing a location for your wholesale business, warehousing needs are a vital consideration, as is projected expansion.

Before Signing a Lease

Unless you're planning to purchase the commercial location, rent your location from a family member or accept a temporary agreement in a location that is for sale. But keep in mind that you will be required to sign a lease before moving in. The most desirable agreement for you as a new business owner is a one- to two-year lease with a renewal option and a guaranteed rate for rent increases over a five- to ten-year period.

Rent for a commercial location is established either on a flat rate or a percentage basis. Under the flat rate, rent is generally based on the square footage of the shop and on the location or, in some cases, on potential volume. The percentage base involves a base amount of rent plus a prearranged percentage of monthly sales.

Your lease will also cover a number of other points, such as the liabilities and responsibilities of the landlord and of you, the tenant; i.e., who is to pay for utilities, specific repairs, renovations, tax increases, etc.

The lease may contain stipulations about the size of the exterior sign you can erect, hours of operation, insurance coverage, and assignation of the lease to another party (a sublet).

Before signing a lease to set up your business, make sure that electrical lines are adequate enough to handle high-volume usage, that you have restrooms for employees and/or clients, and that there are convenient parking areas. Also check with the leasing agent to be certain you can make leasehold improvements, e.g., storage shelves, at your discretion as the business warrants it.

It is recommended that you have an attorney review the lease carefully before you sign it to ensure you understand all of the clauses and to serve as a negotiator, if necessary.

Review

If setting up my business at home, I have

- ◆ Checked with the city and county offices in my area regarding required licenses and permits and zoning regulations for the home office _____
- ◆ Set aside a room or an area in my home that will be used exclusively for my business _____
- ◆ Installed a separate telephone line and purchased an answering machine, or contracted with an answering service _____
- ◆ Set up a separate business bank account _____
- ◆ Informed friends and family of my business routine and specific working hours to reduce interruptions and distractions _____

If setting up in a commercial location, I have

- ◆ Investigated rental rates for the area I am interested in leasing _____
- ◆ Checked traffic flow, parking, and foot traffic around my proposed location _____
- ◆ Determined that my business is compatible with others in the area _____
- ◆ Talked with my prospective landlord about improvements, maintenance, and rent increases _____
- ◆ Had my attorney check the rental agreement and any local zoning regulations _____
- ◆ Secured the necessary operating licenses and permits from the city and/or county _____

Notes

Key Points

Possible Locations

Size and Floor Plan Considerations

9

PROFESSIONAL BACKUP

From the start-up stage and as your business continues to grow and prosper, you will need the assistance of several professionals, including a lawyer, an accountant, and an insurance agent.

The best way to find a professional is, according to the majority of business owners, through personal recommendations from other entrepreneurs, especially those in similar businesses as yours, and from friends or relatives. The most important factor is that the person doing the recommending understand exactly what you will need from the professional you will be hiring.

For example, your cousin's divorce lawyer is probably not as well suited to helping you draw up a partnership agreement as the attorney a friend used for help with incorporating his business.

Before making a decision, talk to several recommended professionals until you find someone who can best satisfy your needs for the business as outlined below and who has a fee structure you can afford.

Equally important: Your choice should be someone you feel comfortable with, especially during periods when you find yourself having to call several times a week to resolve a problem or complete a specific task.

In many cases, because attorneys and accountants often work on a particular business matter in conjunction with one

another, the attorney you select may be able to suggest an account-
ant who can properly service your business, or vice versa.

If you're planning to hire an attorney or an accountant, you
should start interviewing likely candidates eight to nine months
prior to the date you plan to start the business. This will give you
time to find a suitable match and give the attorney time to take
care of all pre-start-up functions, such as assisting in the structure
of your business or helping with your business plan.

Professional Services

Legal

An attorney with broad-based expertise in business can help you
with such matters as raising capital; the legal and tax ramifications
and benefits of various business forms including sole proprietor-
ship, partnership, or corporation; name clearance to ensure that
you are not using a name already designated by another company;
legal tips on operating in your desired location; and help you file
all necessary legal papers and documents needed for financing,
establishing your business form, and so on.

He or she will review contracts and lease agreements and can
provide support with collection problems. The lawyer you select
should also be willing and able to represent you in the event of
any claims that are brought against you or lawsuits you initiate.

Laws Dictating Mail Order

The bottom line is that your responsibilities to the mail order
shopper are dictated by law. The sad truth is that mail order fraud
occurs to the tune of over $50 million a year lost by customers.

Recent Postal Service figures showed that, in one year, there
were 142,000 complaints about mail order fraud in the United
States. Most of these complaints involve

- ♦ Orders that are never received
- ♦ Orders that are not completely filled
- ♦ Orders that arrive damaged
- ♦ Orders that don't work as advertised

♦ Failure to honor money-back guarantees

You and your attorney need to be aware of the regulations of the Federal Trade Commission (FTC) and other regulatory agencies, some of which follow:

1. ***Truth in advertising.*** This means that you cannot misrepresent your products or business to the consumer. You must make prices absolutely and perfectly clear so there is no confusion on the part of the buyer. Advertising copy and art must present a clear and truthful interpretation of the product.

2. ***Deliveries.*** Products must be delivered within the time you say they will be. If you don't specify a time limit, the merchandise must be received by the customer within thirty days of the date you receive the order. If a problem arises that prevents you from honoring this rule, you are required to write the buyer and give the option of a refund. If the customer requests a refund, you must send it within seven days of receipt of the request. If the item was charged, the refund must be credited within one billing cycle.

The FTC can and will take mail order violators to court. Fines for violations run up to $10,000 a day. To make sure you're absolutely clear on the FTC's regulations, send for a copy of the Mail Order Rule (and any other appropriate pamphlets) from

> The Federal Trade Commission
> Division of Legal and Public Records
> Washington, DC 20580

Fees

Depending on your lawyer's expertise, reputation, and the market he or she serves (metropolitan area versus small town, for example), fees will differ dramatically.

In a small community, lawyers often charge a set rate for the job being done, while "city" lawyers typically charge by the hour with fees ranging anywhere from $65 to $250 per hour.

This does not include the extraneous expenses involved, such as the $300 to $1,000 cost of incorporating (depending on the state you operate in). Neither do these fees include supplemental costs, such as travel and telephone, incurred by the attorney in the handling of your case.

A good way to determine the range of fees in your area is to check with your local chamber of commerce or the state bar association, generally located in the capital city. The bar association may also be able to provide you with information about a particular attorney's reputation and expertise.

When talking with potential attorneys—and when you have found one who is compatible with your needs—always be sure to ask for an outline of expenses and if he or she is willing to notify you when the fees for a particular task will be exceeded.

Accounting

The accountant you select should, early on, be able to work with you on assembling your business plan, including your projected profit and loss statements, for financing.

Down the line, as your business is being established, the accountant will help you set up your books and, once in operation, should handle your tax returns, prepare financial statements, and offer financial advice regarding tax matters, cash flow, investments to maximize the use of profits, and the tax regulations regarding employees when you are ready to hire.

Fees

As with attorneys, there is a professional association in your state capital that certifies and maintains records on the reputation and fee structures of accountants.

The basis for fee structuring does vary slightly, however, with accountants. Some charge by the hour, others by the day, and still others work on a set monthly retainer based on the estimated amount of time they will be required to spend on your work.

Be prepared, however, to pay hourly fees that average between $25 and $100, depending on the accountant's expertise and location.

Insurance

Before setting out on your search for an insurance agent, it is advisable to have already established your business form and learned exactly what insurance the law in your area requires you to carry (fire, liability, etc.) and, if hiring employees, what kind of program you'll be offering employees, as well as your own needs for medical and life insurance.

There are several types of insurance you should carry for your mail order company. General business coverage will protect against fire and theft, general liability covers accidents or injury to anyone while on your work premises, and product liability covers anyone getting hurt with one of your products. If working out of your home, it may be possible to add these additional types of coverage to your existing homeowner's policy at a low annual cost.

You will need to carry workers' compensation when you start hiring full- or part-time employees, unless they agree to work as independent contractors and take care of their own insurance and taxes.

The insurance agent you choose should be familiar with the needs of businesses and business owners, not just the standard life and disability policies. Your insurance needs will change as your business grows and expands (i.e., employee health, workers' compensation, etc.). At that point, you may want to consider key-person coverage to ensure that your company can survive if a major partner or employee dies.

There are also a number of pension programs and stock-option programs available in the event you want to offer employees the incentive to increase their participation in the company in exchange for partial "ownership" down the line.

Fees

The fees for your agent's expertise are paid from your premiums, and there should be no extra charge for advice or administration of your insurance policies and programs.

Professional Services

Legal

Accounting

Insurance

10

TAXES, LICENSES, AND PERMITS

As a business owner, you are responsible for timely filing and payment of federal, state, and local taxes. Whether you have an accountant prepare your returns or you do it yourself, the task will be made much easier if you establish a systematic record-keeping system (as described in Chapter 14) and keep your records accurate and up to date.

This includes maintaining all written documents pertaining to the financial aspect of your business: invoices, bank statements, receipts of any and all business expenses, and deposit slips.

One of the easiest ways to keep control of the "paper dragon" is to set up a 9 x 12-inch manila envelope or a file folder for each of the following categories:

♦ *Paid Bills*–both personal and business

♦ *Sales Receipts* of every product you've sold or service job you've performed

♦ *Inventory* records based on ongoing inventory control and quarterly audits

♦ *Copies of Invoices* or billing statements that are paid, with a separate file for those still due you

♦ **Receipts** for miscellaneous cash purchases

♦ **Auto/Entertainment** receipts from travel and promotional activities

All of these documents must be kept for at least five years to substantiate deductions claimed on your income tax returns in the event of an Internal Revenue Service (IRS) audit. Make up new file folders or envelopes at the beginning of each year and store the old ones in a safe place.

Preparing income tax returns is not only a time-consuming task that can take you away from the important job of running your business, but also somewhat of an art form. Tax law is a constantly changing, complicated fact of life. It is strongly recommended that you have an accountant lined up to prepare your taxes and to keep you informed of any pertinent changes during the year.

Business Deductions

The deductions that you will most likely qualify for as a business owner include operating expenses such as telephone, postage, advertising, bank service charges, travel and expense of conventions, interest, dues to professional organizations, and subscriptions to magazines pertaining to your business, among others.

Operating your business from home allows you to deduct not only a substantial portion of your rent or mortgage payment, but also percentages of your phone and utility expenses.

If you have established your business at home, you will be able to deduct that portion of the house used exclusively for business, as well as a percentage of your costs for telephone service and utilities.

Again, because of the complexity and obscurity of many of the deductions, it is best to have a professional prepare your taxes

to ensure you get the full benefits to which you are entitled. Filing requirements will be determined by the type of business, the legal structure (sole proprietorship, partnership, or corporation), income from the business, your location, state and local laws, and whether or not you have employees.

For example, as the sole proprietor of your business you would probably only be required to file personal federal and state returns based on profit or loss, with the appropriate schedules for business expenses, pay scales, self-employment and estimated taxes, and local business license fees and sales taxes.

State Income Tax

Each state has corresponding filing requirements; however, form and schedule numbers vary. Contact your state franchise tax board or your accountant for details.

Local Taxes

Taxes will vary from city to city and county to county; however, you *may* be required to pay city income tax and local sales tax as well as real or personal property taxes. Check with your local government offices for specifics.

Licenses and Permits

To operate your business, you will need permits and licenses based on the requirements in your area and the type of business you are operating. You will probably be required to obtain the following documents regardless of where you live.

Local Business License

Basically, this is simply a fee paid to the city or county where you are located that allows you to operate your business in that area. Some cities will also require you to pay a percentage of your gross sales every year.

Fictitious Name Statement

This is a registration for protection of your business name. Filing the fictitious name statement will also involve a city- or county-wide search to make sure you are not duplicating an existing name. This can be done at your county hall of records. (See details in Chapter 11.)

Seller's Permit or Resale Certificate

This is required only if you are going to be charging sales tax. Services are often exempt.

Health Permit

This is required only if you are preparing or distributing food in any manner, and involves an initial inspection and periodic follow-up inspections by health department officials.

Taxpayer Identification Number

This is available from the IRS in the case of partnerships, Subchapter S corporations, or corporations. Sole proprietors are required to have a taxpayer identification number if they pay wages to one or more employees or file pension or excise tax forms.

Your local governmental offices or your attorney will be able to give you specific licenses and permits required, as well as the corresponding fees for each as they apply to your business.

Legal Structure

As a self-employed business owner, you are required to decide on a legal form of business for tax reporting purposes. There are four basic classifications, as outlined below. If, after reviewing them, you are still unsure of which way to go, it would be advisable to talk with a lawyer about the advantages and disadvantages of each structure for your particular business.

All businesses, regardless of size, are required to maintain detailed records and file the necessary tax returns. In a corporation, regular meetings must be held. The stockholders elect a board of directors, who establish and monitor corporate policy. The board

selects corporate officers to conduct the day-to-day operations of the business.

Sole proprietorships are the most convenient and least complicated form of organization for new business owners, especially in the early stages. As your business grows, you will want to explore the options as a way of protecting your personal assets and increasing the potential for expansion capital.

Sole Proprietorship

This is the easiest to establish and is the structure many small business owners choose. A proprietorship is relatively free from government regulation, as the business has no existence apart from the owner. Profits from the operation of the business are treated as personal income for purposes of taxation, and your proprietary interest ends when you die or dissolve the business.

The major drawback of a proprietorship is that you are personally liable for any and all claims against the business and undertake the risks of the business to the extent of all assets, whether they are used in the business or personally owned. As a sole proprietor, you will be required to file self-employment tax returns and ordinarily would have to make estimated tax payments on a quarterly basis.

General Partnership

This is also an easy structure to set up and administer. Since responsibilities and capitalization are usually shared by two or more partners, taxation is based on each partner's share of business income and determined by their individual tax rates. Again, claims against the business can be filed against personal assets, and financial liability is shared equally by all partners.

Limited Partnership

This structure can be established when one or more people are willing to invest cash or tangible property in the business with active participation in the daily operations. However, there must be at least one general partner who carries unlimited financial

liability and who usually maintains a full-time managerial position within the company.

The limited partners are only liable for business debts up to the amount of their investment. Although a partnership is not a taxable entity, it must figure its profit or loss and file an annual tax return, which also becomes part of the partners' personal returns.

Corporation

In this structure, stock or shares in the business are sold to investors or stockholders, who then control the company. The advantage is that corporate stockholders are removed from any liability against personal assets. The most anyone can lose in the event of bankruptcy or a liability claim is his or her stock.

The privilege of reduced liability, however, creates paperwork (articles of incorporation and annual reports for the state tax commission and federal regulators), expenses (filing and licensing fees), and double taxation (the corporation is taxed on profits, while stockholders and elected officers are taxed individually on wages and/or dividend income).

Subchapter S Corporations

This structure has proved to be a real boon for small business owners who want the benefit of corporate protection from personal liability without double taxation. In a Subchapter S corporation, a maximum of thirty-five stockholders (who can be family members) report their share of corporate income on individual tax returns.

The corporation itself is generally exempt from federal income tax; however, it may be required to pay a tax on excess net passive investment income, capital gains, or built-in gains. To structure your company as a Subchapter S corporation, all of the shareholders must consent to the choice.

Notes

Key Points

Personal Thoughts

Additional Research

11

NAMING YOUR BUSINESS

As a pet owner, it is unlikely that you would give your German shepherd a name like Fifi. It wouldn't suit the dog's image, nor would it be appropriate. The same principle applies to choosing a name for your business.

The name you select for your business can be a tremendous asset when it defines the kind of image you want to project. You want the name to attract and appeal to potential customers, to be easily remembered over that of the competition's, and appropriate to the type of business you are starting.

Today's consumers are constantly bombarded with advertising as they go about their daily routines. Getting their attention, and holding it long enough for them to make an association between your business name and what you are offering, is imperative.

A memorable moniker can mean the difference between continued growth or a mediocre response from an audience victimized by information overload. (It is important to remember that your ultimate success depends on well-designed advertising, careful planning, and quality products and/or service.)

*Historically, in developing business names, simplicity
has scored the highest points. The name you choose
should be short, to the point, and easy for
consumers to pronounce.*

Many small business owners claim their image is enhanced by the
use of a straightforward name that conveys their business concept
but maintains a sense of personal identity—a factor that is espe-
cially important in today's high-tech world.

As an example, when Susan Hopper made the decision to
open a preschool, she grappled with names like The ABC Center,
Kiddie Land, and Now We Are Three. Finally, out of exasperation
and because she felt these selections were either inappropriate or
too cute, she decided to go with Susan's School, feeling it was easy
to remember and conveyed exactly the personal, homey atmos-
phere she wanted to create. She claims that 50 percent of the
parents who have picked her preschool for their children from the
telephone book did so because it sounded friendly and sincere.

Naming Your Mail Order Business

Take some time to think about this, because your company name
needs to fulfill several functions beyond identifying you.

The name you choose can

- ◆ Influence a customer's perceptions of your legitimacy

- ◆ Determine whether or not you have to get a special city,
 state, or county license to operate your business

- ◆ Affect your ad costs; the shorter the name, the less you
 pay. And at $4-$8 a word, it adds up

The selected name shouldn't be so exclusive that you can't sell
other products under the same name when you expand. All things
considered, it is probably best to just use your own name followed
by "company," "enterprises," "products" or the like. It leaves room
to grow. And, unless your name utilizes every letter in the alphabet
more than once, your ad costs will be that much lower.

If you do not want to name the business after yourself, be sure that what you do come up with is catchy enough to stand above your competitors, appeals both to the eye and ear, and is general enough to avoid being limiting: Associated Enterprises, Bay Area Distributors, Western Products, and so on. Start by making a list of all the positive aspects of your business that you can think of, and call on friends and relatives to provide as many ideas as they can.

Brainstorming

Start by making a list of all the positive aspects of your business that you can think of, and call on friends and relatives to provide as many as they can come up with. Write down all the possibilities, no matter how funny or unusual they seem. A handy tool for business naming is the thesaurus, which will give you a vast number of options for commonplace names. Consider everything that springs forth from your imagination.

When you have created a list of likely candidates, get together with a group of supportive friends and family members and have a brainstorming session to either pick one of the choices you have come up with or to develop something from the ideas listed. Chances are that within a few hours, you will have a name for your business. Catchy names are fun to design. However, make sure it isn't so offbeat, cute, or trendy as to risk slipping into obscurity as time passes.

...And an Address

In addition to choosing a name, you need to decide about an address. There are two schools of thought here: One is that it's preferable to have a post office box rather than use your home address. Boxes are tax deductible, help keep your address short in ads, and keep things simple if you move within the same area.

On the other hand, customers may respond more positively to a street address because it lends a certain sense of trustworthiness. Perhaps in your area there is a private postal box service that provides addresses like, "Jane Q. Public, 2323 Main Street, Suite 22, Anytown." These are great because they are boxes that look

like street addresses. They are, however, more expensive than U.S. Postal Service boxes.

The Fictitious Name Statement

You are required to file a fictitious name statement with the county clerk's office where you will be basing the business. While there, you should be able to do a countywide name check on the spot to see if there are any other businesses in the region using the name you have selected. The filing fee depends on where you live, and must be done within thirty days after you officially open your business.

It will also be necessary to publish the fictitious name in a local newspaper; the cost depends on the circulation of the paper. The county clerk's office will advise you about specific requirements in your area.

If you are starting a business that will be operating in a broader market, statewide or nationally, it is important to have your attorney do a name clearance investigation, which can take from three days to three weeks.

Your Visual Image

After you have selected a name that reflects your business image, the next step is translating it into a visual symbol or logo (logotype) to serve as the signature piece for your business. Often this involves creating a visual interpretation of your company name, but in other cases a graphic symbol or trademark is designed to serve as identification.

Some established corporate trademarks are so familiar that you can immediately identify the company even without seeing or hearing its name.

A good example of this includes the logo of the dog with his head cocked to one side. The accompanying copy reads "His Master's Voice," and it's a good bet that you recognize this as the logo for RCA. Another effective logo is the avant-garde apple that identifies Apple computer products.

If you do not have the graphic skills necessary to design a logo with impact, get in touch with your nearest art association

(listed in the phone book or available through local art supply shops or galleries) or call a nearby college or university. Ask the head of the art department if your design can be given as a class assignment or if he or she could recommend a student to do the job for a small fee. It will give students practical application, and the design can be used later in their portfolio. You can offer cash or a prize for the best design. The students will undoubtedly meet the challenge with enthusiasm and give you a number of good samples and ideas from which to choose.

Selecting a Typeface

Save sample logos and advertisements that use a typeface you like. Type is an extremely important element of logo design and can also pinpoint the precise image you hope to express. Type not only presents the basic message, it can play a powerful role in the overall appearance of your logo and can actually create atmosphere. A chart of some of the more popular typefaces is included at the end of this chapter.

When deciding on a typeface for your logo, visit print shops or typesetting studios and look at their typeface books. They offer both the usual, functional varieties as well as a selection of unique typefaces that can really dress up your logo and subtly portray a specific personality such as dignified, fun, powerful, classic, or cutting edge.

Have the logo and your business information (address, phone number, etc.) set in more than the one typeface so that you can see how they will look when printed. Also ask to have them set in both small (10- to 12-point for business cards) and larger (20- to 24-point for letterhead) versions. Once typeset, you will be able to make a final decision about which typeface suits the image you want to project.

Typesetters generally have a minimum fee based on the amount of time they spend on a job, which can vary from $15 per hour in a small city to $50 per hour in a business area, as high as $100 per hour in major metropolitan areas. That's why it's important to shop around.

Word processing specialists or independent desktop publishers can also provide a variety of typefaces and formats at less

expense. Since you will only be having a few words typeset, the time and cost required to set them in several different styles should certainly be affordable.

Business Cards and Stationery

The typeface and logo you eventually choose will be used on your letterhead; in your display and telephone advertising; on all promotional materials, including flyers, brochures, and announcements; on your sign; and on statements and invoices.

They will also be used on your business cards, one of the most inexpensive and convenient ways to inform people about your service or product. Once you have had cards printed, be generous. Give one to everyone you meet and always be sure to carry a supply wherever you go.

Most fast-print copy centers are prepared to help you if you decide not to design your own business cards and stationery. They have samples of business forms, letterheads, and cards with various styles to choose from. Make sure that your company name, logo, address, and phone number are included where necessary. If you have a fax and/or toll-free number, be sure those numbers are included. When someone looks at your card or letterhead, it must tell them instantly who you are, what your business is, and how you can be reached.

Sample Fonts

Helvetica
ABCDEFGHIJ
abcdefghij

Helvetica Black
ABCDEFGHIJ
abcdefghij

Helvetica Condensed
ABCDEFGHIJ
abcdefghij

ITC Eras
ABCDEFGHIJ
abcdefghij

ITC Eras Demi
ABCDEFGHIJ
abcdefghij

ITC Eras Bold
ABCDEFGHIJ
abcdefghij

Korinna
ABCDEFGHIJ
abcdefghij

Korinna Bold
ABCDEFGHIJ
abcdefghij

Rose Round
ABCDEFGHIJ
abcdefghij

Lubalin Graph
ABCDEFGHIJ
abcdefghij

Britannic Light
ABCDEFGHIJ
abcdefghij

Britannic Bold
ABCDEFGHIJ
abcdefghij

Brush Script
ABCDEFGHIJ
abcdefghij

Optima
ABCDEFGHIJ
abcdefghij

Optima Italic
ABCDEFGHIJ
abcdefghij

Optima Bold
ABCDEFGHIJ
abcdefghij

Park Avenue
ABCDEFGHIJ
abcdefghij

Palatino
ABCDEFGHIJ
abcdefghij

Palatino Italic
ABCDEFGHIJ
abcdefghij

Palatino Bold
ABCDEFGHIJ
abcdefghij

Garamond Book
ABCDEFGHIJ
abcdefghij

Garamond Ultra
ABCDEFGHIJ
abcdefghij

Times Roman
ABCDEFGHIJ
abcdefghij

Times Italic
ABCDEFGHIJ
abcdefghij

ITC Fenice Regular
ABCDEFGHIJ
abcdefghij

ITC Fenice Bold
ABCDEFGHIJ
abcdefghij

ITC Fenice Ultra
ABCDEFGHIJ
abcdefghij

Eurostile
ABCDEFGHIJ
abcdefghij

Eurostile Bold
ABCDEFGHIJ
abcdefghij

Eurostile Extended
ABCDEFGHIJ
abcdefghij

Notes

Key Points

Personal Thoughts

Additional Research

12

DEVELOPING A BUSINESS PLAN

Developing your business plan is the most important process you will undertake in your career as an entrepreneur, regardless of the size or type of business you have decided to start.

A well-thought-out business plan will serve as a blueprint while your idea turns into a recognizable entity and as it grows into a stable and profitable venture. Too often we hear former small business owners say they probably could have made a success of their business if they had only known what to expect from the beginning...and that is where the business plan comes in.

Unfortunately, too many new entrepreneurs are unfamiliar with the importance of planning, or consider themselves an exception and feel they can succeed by winging it or dealing with problems as they arise. Not true!

Every business, whether a large commercial venture or a small home-based enterprise, needs to analyze its potential, examine its strengths and weaknesses, and determine the future of the organization. It works for the major corporations and it will work for you, especially once you become involved in the day-to-day operations of the business. Having a business plan will give you the freedom to follow the steps you have carefully laid out with regard to budgeting, the success ratio of your product or service, the hiring of employees, and other growth decisions.

Advantages of the Business Plan

Once you have made the decision to become a business owner, you must devise a specific statement that clearly outlines *what* you plan to do, *when* you plan to do it, and *how* you will accomplish the short- and long-term goals.

Not only will this keep you on track, it will serve as an indicator to others of your sincerity and knowledge when you go out to find start-up or expansion capital, and it will serve as the foundation of your financing proposal.

The other advantage is that the actual task of putting your business plan together will help you define and clarify every step of your concept and, if done in a conscientious and objective manner, will point out potential trouble spots that can be addressed before they become major problems.

If all the necessary components are covered, it will put your business on the road to profit. It is a sure bet that, down the road, if you find your business is not generating the income you had originally projected, this is because you didn't include one or more of the basic business plan requirements.

Not a Guessing Game

Like any other major project, preparing a business plan involves time and research. It shouldn't be a guessing game. It will be necessary to ask yourself some very specific questions and to answer them thoughtfully and honestly. The business plan is your foundation, so build it carefully to ensure that it works at optimum efficiency for your needs. And make sure it is typed, orderly, and good looking so that you and others can recognize its importance in the professional scheme of your expanding operation.

An important aspect to remember is that your business plan is not cast in stone. In fact, what makes a business plan so great is that it invites revisions as your business changes and grows. This makes it a companion in your success and, by reviewing it regularly, a partner in your progress.

Work Tip

Plan ahead. Allow yourself plenty of time to handle all of the tasks involved with marketing a mail order product. Set up concise work schedules using weekly and monthly planning calendars, and create lists to be sure you do everything that must be done. This includes scheduling the design and placement of advertising for different publications, arranging inventory, and planning for boxing and shipping of goods after the orders are received.

The best way to approach your business plan is to take paper and pen and devote a few hours to coming up with some hard answers. Of course, you will want to condense your answers to fit into specific segments within the plan, including (in order of appearance) Concept and Feasibility, Legal Structure, Product or Service, Customer Base, Marketing and Production Goals, Personnel (your résumé and Entrepreneurial Profile and those of any other key personnel), and Financial Statements.

It is advisable to start each segment on a separate page and to create a table of contents to place in the front. Be sure it is well-written and organized, neatly typed, and bound in a report folder to preserve it and give it a professional look, especially when using it as a sales tool to convince lenders.

Key Questions to Ask Yourself

The first question you must ask yourself is: "Why am I interested in this particular business?" Probably the answer will be something to the effect of wanting to be your own boss and making money...independence and income.

This answer is fine as a personal goal, but it isn't going to be good enough if you are planning to approach potential lenders for funding. They will want to see an overview of your business concept, why you are convinced it will be successful, and where it fits in the scheme of similar businesses in your town or city.

The next question you must ask is: "What is my product or service?" This may seem like a ridiculous question since you know your product is gift baskets or your service is catering, local sightseeing tours, or whatever, but it goes deeper. Your written response will include details about the service or a description of your product (preferably positive), with a focus on why customers will be inclined to work with you.

Additional questions to consider should include

- ♦ Why do I believe there is a need for my product or service?
- ♦ How do I plan to develop my business over the next five years?
- ♦ How much will I charge to ensure value to the customer and profit for myself?
- ♦ Who are my suppliers?
- ♦ Who are my customers?
- ♦ What equipment do I need to start the business?
- ♦ How much inventory and supplies do I need for start-up?
- ♦ What will it cost?
- ♦ Who are my competitors and where are they located?
- ♦ What does the competition offer and how will I offer something different to attract customers?
- ♦ What changes are occurring in my marketing area that will impact my business in the future?
- ♦ What are my estimated sales figures for each of the next five years? (A guesstimate can be based on researching similar businesses in the area.)
- ♦ How will I advertise and promote my business and how will I pay for it?
- ♦ How and where is my product going to be manufactured?
- ♦ What is involved in the production—materials, labor, costs?
- ♦ Where will my service be performed?

♦ What equipment is required for my service and what are the costs for leasing versus purchasing?

♦ What are other overhead expenses (rent, employees, etc.)?

♦ How many people will be involved in the business and what are their qualifications?

♦ If I don't have employees, am I qualified to run the business myself?

By talking with people in similar businesses, suppliers, direct competitors, and your local chamber of commerce, you will gather a great deal of information, both positive and negative, about your potential business. People love to talk about their success and, if you ask in the right way, their failures.

If you operate like an investigative reporter for a few days while doing research for your business plan, it's guaranteed that you will obtain plenty of good, solid information. A Service Corps of Retired Executives (SCORE) representative through the Small Business Administration can also provide assistance or tell you about resources that can help you develop a realistic business plan.

Trade associations, listed in reference books available at your local library, can provide you with invaluable details on industry facts and figures, such as the percentage of gross sales that should be spent on advertising, the percentage that is typically paid for rent in your particular business, and how to price your product or service.

The final item to include in this section of your business plan, when and if presenting it for financing, is a personal résumé, designed to emphasize your general business management experience and your expertise within your specific area.

Describe the job duties for every job you have held, including any special aspects that pertain directly to the business.

If you cannot prepare the résumé, it is worth the minor fee to have it done professionally. The results will pay for the cost hundreds of times over.

Show me a person with an obsession about succeeding and a solid business plan, and I'll show you a good risk.

Anonymous Loan Officer

Financial Statements

Once you have written your overview and description sheets, it's time to get down to numbers. This is the key to your business plan and, unfortunately, the area where many entrepreneurs get bogged down. But without an understanding about the numbers involved, you can never expect to be a good manager and really shouldn't be surprised if you run into money problems within the first year.

Again, utilizing the resources indicated above—chamber of commerce, trade associations—you will need to work up your financial pages to include the following components, which most lenders will want to see projected for one and five years.

Projected operating expenses. This projected number includes materials, advertising, salaries for employees or outside labor, and other expenses directly related to the cost of doing business.

Estimate of gross (before tax) sales revenue. If the business is not yet operating, base your estimate on research figures from trade associations and what the local market dictates. If business is underway, base your estimate on how many items or hours of service you plan to sell and the average price you plan to charge.

How you arrived at the figures for these statements. Generally, you would base your figures on assumptions made about the number of months of operation, estimated number of sales, and the average amount versus the cost of each sale.

Cost of equipment and furnishings. Get estimated quotes, whether you are planning to purchase or lease these items.

Cost of materials. You need to know how much items will cost for production, if applicable, and for maintenance on equipment needed to run the business.

Additional operating expenses. You should research prices for rent, telephone and other utilities, business taxes and license fees, office supplies, and even decorating costs. Include a category called "other" to provide a cushion for unexpected expenses.

Balance sheet. This shows assets, such as equipment and operating capital you already have, and liabilities or debts and expenses. If the business has not yet started, this would be a personal balance sheet indicating your net worth, listing all possessions of any value plus cash, stock, and other holdings, minus financial responsibilities.

Leasehold improvements. If you are planning to rent a commercial location or redesign a room within your home strictly for business, estimate cleaning and restoration costs in this statement.

By investing the time and energy into this portion of the business plan, you will absorb the numbers into your consciousness and be able to recognize, at a glance, when your costs exceed your profit margin or when you are in a position to start expanding.

If money matters are absolutely beyond your comprehension at this point, it would pay to hire someone to work with you to develop the financial pages of the plan. There are business consultants and accountants who will probably charge you a substantial amount, or you can approach the accounting or business department of the nearest college and see if there is a qualified student available to help you.

No matter who you find to assist you, however, be sure to stay involved in the process...the discipline and hard work will guarantee success.

Notes

Key Points

Personal Thoughts

Additional Research

13

FINANCING YOUR BUSINESS

Starting your business without having sufficient capital is setting yourself up for problems from the beginning. Undercapitalization is cited as one of the major reasons why businesses do not succeed; however, this simply boils down to bad planning.

If you research and record all the goals, marketing data, equipment and supply requirements, and financial needs of your venture before actually opening your doors, you will be able to see at a glance how much you need to get going, and *why you need it.* That way, there will be no surprises and no reason that your business should suffer from lack of capitalization.

It is important to have the financial resources to cover all your preliminary planning and start-up costs, including expenses incurred to research the feasibility of your business and expenses required to set up shop, from equipment and supplies to advertising and utility setup charges. In addition, you need a surplus to carry you over personally until the business becomes productive. The Cash Flow Statement, Start-up Costs Worksheet, and Projected Expense Statement forms provided in Chapter 5 will help you determine these expenses.

If, after developing your business plan (Chapter 12), you find that your personal resources are not enough to open the business, there are other options available.

The four most common methods include

♦ Starting the business on a part-time basis while holding a full-time job to cover expenses

♦ Taking on a limited partner

♦ Going to friends or family members for the money you need

♦ Applying for a loan through a commercial lender or the Small Business Administration (SBA)

There are, of course, pros and cons to each of these options.

Starting Out Part-time

Starting your business on a part-time or "moonlighting" basis is a decision that must be made based on the nature of the business. If you are planning to capitalize on your skills in upholstering, for example, you should have no trouble building up the business at night and on weekends.

It is perfectly feasible to start small, using your garage or a spare room as your production facility and purchasing an answering machine for potential customers to leave a message while you are at your regular job. When you get home, you simply call them back to discuss prices and arrange a time when it is convenient to pick up the piece of furniture to be upholstered.

On the other hand, if you are planning to start a temporary help agency, for example, it would be in your best interest to go into it on a full-time, dedicated basis, as your potential customers are going to want fast results and will call someone else if they are even slightly discouraged, such as getting a recorded message when they call.

Moonlighting will work with some businesses, but before exploring it as an option you must figure out if your limited availability will affect your credibility, if you really have the time and energy to work at a regular job and try to build a business (not to mention family responsibilities), and whether your ultimate goal is to be self-employed or just to earn a few extra dollars to supplement your base income.

Considering a Partner

A limited partner is one who will put up the money you need and step into the background to let you run the business the way you see fit. You must be sure, however, to have your attorney draw up a precise partnership agreement that covers every eventuality. Partnerships are typically entered into with the best intentions and the unwavering belief that the business will be successful.

Since this is not always the case—and even if it were—it is a businesslike move to ensure that such aspects as decision making, distribution of profits and losses, contributions of partners, and handling disputes and changes are outlined and approved by all the partners.

Approaching a Lender

Once you have your business plan and other paperwork prepared, decide which lending association you want to approach. Certainly, if you have a stable record with a checking or savings account at your regular bank or savings and loan, that is the place to try first. Set up an appointment with the bank manager or loan officer to make your request and explain why you feel your business venture is worth the bank's investment.

Be aware, however, that banks are more likely to provide you with a loan payable within five or ten years, as opposed to savings and loans, which are more interested in long-term loans, such as for mortgages. Credit unions operate in a similar manner to banks; however, you generally have to be a member. If you do belong to a credit union it could be your best bet, as it offers lower interest rates and can be more flexible in lending decisions.

If, for some reason, you do not want to run a loan through your bank, consider talking with other local small business owners. Very often, they can steer you to a regional, often independently owned bank or savings and loan that is empathetic to and supportive of new businesses. In that case, proceed as mentioned earlier and arrange a meeting with the manager or loan officer.

Present your case in a friendly yet professional manner. Be realistic and honest about your needs. Do not underbid because

you worry that you will not get a loan if you ask for too much. It is always better to start with a higher figure than you actually need so you have a strong negotiating edge.

In addition, most lenders have a pretty good idea about start-up and operating costs of new businesses and are much less likely to give you, and risk losing, a small loan for a business they know calls for more capital. They will be more willing to work with you if you are realistic and knowledgeable about your needs.

If, after your first try, the answer is no, ask for reasons why you are being turned down so you can restructure your presentation. Turn rejection into a learning tool to redefine and polish your material and to develop new negotiating strategies. There are always other lenders you can approach, and the law of averages dictates that you will get your loan if the idea is solid and it is apparent that you have researched the feasibility of starting a business in your particular area.

Money brings some happiness. But, after a certain point, it just brings more money.

Neil Simon

Financing Methods

"Friendly Financing"

The third option, raising capital through friends or family members, is probably one of the methods most often used. The advantage of getting a loan from a personal contact is that he or she knows you, undoubtedly trusts your ability to make the business go, and won't require much in the way of substantiating paperwork, such as complex loan applications, financial statements, etc. In addition, you will most likely be able to negotiate a very low interest rate on the loan.

The major disadvantage, according to entrepreneurs who have taken this route, is if the friendly lender decides that he or she wants to provide input on the care and maintenance of your

business. This problem, however, can be eliminated by a thorough business discussion prior to accepting the loan. In other words, choose your investor carefully!

The second problem has to do with repayment of the loan. Even though you have a loose agreement in writing with your lender, because of friendship or family ties there may come a point when Uncle Bill needs that $10,000 *tomorrow* to take care of a personal obligation. You can't possibly come up with the money overnight, Uncle Bill gets angry, and that whole side of the family turns against you.

The flip side of the coin is if the business fails and you are unable to pay Uncle Bill the $10,000 he put up. There are any number of unpleasant situations, so you must be sure in the beginning to think about the importance of the relationship you have with the potential lender, how the best and the worst of circumstances would affect your relationship, and whether you then could justify asking for money.

Commercial Lenders

If you are not able to, or if you decide against approaching friends or relatives for financial assistance, the next step is a bank, a savings and loan, or a credit union. Before approaching any of these commercial lenders, you must have carefully developed your business plan, which will include the following documents.

1. A résumé or statement outlining your background and capability to operate the business, plus a similar statement about any key employees or partners in the business.

2. A statement of business and personal goals.

3. A description of the business, including market research for your product or service.

4. Details on how the business is going to be structured (sole proprietorship, partnership, corporation).

5. A projection of profit and loss for a minimum of one year (five years is preferable), which means you will have investigated how similar businesses are doing.

6. An outline of how much money you need–and why–to keep the business solvent and to support yourself and your family for at least a year.

In addition, you will be required to provide a personal balance sheet that lists your assets (real estate, car, valuable personal property) and liabilities (mortgage payments, credit card debts) along with a credit application that outlines your personal financial history, so a determination can be made on your ability to pay back the loan. The lender will follow through by requesting a credit report from an independent agency to help with the decision.

The main point to remember when applying for a loan with a commercial institution is that lenders aren't as concerned about the amount loaned as they are about how and when they are going to get the money back!

Paying Back the Loan

When you apply for financing, the burden of proof as it relates to repayment rests with you. No one would knowingly grant a loan to an individual or a business that he or she had doubts about. As a borrower, your responsibility is to show that you will be able to pay back the loan according to the terms agreed to by you and the lender. If you have a good credit history, a credit report will indicate as much.

The Small Business Administration

The Small Business Administration (SBA) often goes where no other lender will tread and, as such, is a lender of last resort. The SBA is a government agency that is well known for providing financing to entrepreneurs who have been repeatedly turned down by commercial lenders, which, in fact, you generally must be before the SBA will consider backing you.

After your loan request with a commercial institution has been denied, you can file an application with the nearest branch of the SBA. It is a good idea to make an appointment with a Service Corps of Retired Executives (SCORE) representative (a man or woman who volunteers his or her time to the SBA-SCORE program to advise new and established business owners). Your SCORE

representative will lead you through the complex paperwork required by the SBA before it makes a decision.

In addition, SCORE volunteers are usually straightforward, knowledgeable men and women who will walk through your business plans with you and offer constructive suggestions. Once the paperwork is completed, a commercial lender will make the loan under the SBA Lender Certification Program, knowing that the government is willing to insure it.

We recommend this option only after you have been turned down by three or more banks, because of the time factor involved in gaining approval and also because of the extensive follow-up reports required by the SBA. It is, however, a viable option and one that has helped thousands of dedicated entrepreneurs realize their goals.

Venture Capitalists

Money is available to businesses that are already established and seeking working or expansion capital from groups of investors known as venture capitalists. These groups can vary from a few local businesspeople with money to invest to major investment companies that are connected with large corporations or financial organizations.

Venture capital is not like a straightforward business loan. It is usually dependent on a minimum $100,000 investment and, therefore, is not suited to every business situation. Typically, venture capitalists are interested in companies that have a track record, a proven position in the market, and a solid growth projection.

And, like a bank or other lending association, venture capitalists want to see a written business plan and a prospectus of future projections. They are looking at your background, the market, the kind of funding you want, and your past financial record.

Since venture capitalists are looking to earn from 10 to 15 percent on their investment over a relatively short period, they will want to spend a great deal of time talking with you and your associates, customers, and suppliers.

Before considering venture capital, we advise discussing it carefully with an attorney who can help you investigate different groups to figure out the best investment structure, and who can work with the group's attorney on drawing up an agreement that protects you. Many venture capitalists will want to own part of your company.

This is an option to be considered only when your company is well established and undergoing rapid growth pains and should be approached with great understanding of the situation.

Other Financing Options

Loan Companies

Loan companies are good sources of funding. However, interest rates are high, and they will generally want to have substantial collateral, such as the equity in your house, on record before making a loan.

Insurance Companies

Your insurance carrier may be willing to make an investment in your small business, using your insurance policy as collateral, or you may even have enough cash value in your policy, depending on the face amount, to provide substantial start-up capital. If this is the case, you will only be required to pay quarterly or semiannual interest payments on the cash value you have taken out.

Factoring

In this scenario, a factoring company "buys" your accounts receivable and advances you a percentage of the full amount due. This is a viable option for well-established service companies that work on a billing basis.

Cosigner

If you have a relative or friend who is already an established business owner or, at least, a homeowner with a solid credit rating, it might be worth your while to ask if he or she would cosign on a loan application with you. Although you are still responsible for

repayment of the loan, the bank is assured that, in the event you default for any reason, the cosigner will guarantee the obligation. It is sometimes difficult to find someone who will do this, but again it doesn't hurt to ask, especially if it is a last resort.

Starting Small

Even if you know your particular business is valid and that you have the ability to make it succeed, be certain that your business plan is realistic. If you have chosen to start a business on a grand scale but have minimal capital and little business experience, it may be best to begin a smaller, less elaborate operation at first.

You'll require less "seed money" and will be in a low-risk position while learning the operations of a business and seeing if you can handle all the variables of business ownership while making it grow.

Smaller businesses have proven to be a great way to learn successful methods, as well as a vehicle for ironing out the many small, often overlooked, details. The profits you gain from a smaller venture can be used to expand or invest in bigger business ideas. And an added bonus is that when you are ready to approach investors or lending institutions, you will be able to show them that you already have a solid track record and a working knowledge of business procedures.

*The journey of a thousand miles begins
with a single step.*

Chinese Proverb

What to Do When Asking for Money

1. ***Be sure to ask.*** This may seem like a gross statement of the obvious, but you would be amazed at the number of small business owners we've heard about who never ask because they are afraid of being turned down.

 Unless you are independently wealthy and pursuing your business as a humanitarian effort, it is unlikely that

you are in a position to run your business and earn enough money to support you, your family, and the operation—especially during the first year. Remember the old adage: It *takes* money to *make* money.

If you run a low-budget business, you will probably get a low-budget response. If you are determined to make it work, be sure you have sufficient capital to make it work the right way.

Fear is often a factor: "I don't want to ask, in case I'm told no." Well, that's the worst thing that can happen. But if you persevere and are serious about your venture, someone will inevitably say yes!

And don't overlook friends and family; they can be your most ardent supporters if you have given them reason in the past to believe you are responsible and determined to succeed.

2. ***Know how much you need.*** Lenders are familiar with the financial demands of business operation and will respect your request if you have obviously done your homework and can talk intelligently about your needs.

3. ***Be direct and confident.*** If you believe in your business and in your ability to make it work, others will be convinced as well. Never apologize for mistakes you feel you have made in the past.

 Simply present the facts honestly, even if it includes revealing an error in judgment you have made somewhere along the line, and assure the lender that he or she will be making a smart decision by investing in you.

4. ***Think positively.*** If you need $50,000, ask for $50,000. Never underestimate the potential to provide. Remember: It is easier to negotiate and deal with one lender for a single amount than it is to keep paperwork and relationships strong with several, all of whom have contributed to the pot.

5. ***Ask again.*** If they trusted you once and you have lived up to the stipulations of the contract, ask again—that goes for commercial lending institutions as well as friends and

relatives. When it comes to borrowing money, a proven record is what it's all about, and if you have established yours, keep it active. It will be your passport to profit when the chips are down.

6. ***Know when to borrow.*** If you have worked out your business plan and know you can survive while getting the business off the ground, start exploring your financing options ahead of time. Don't wait until the last minute when you will be forced to act and will have to take a less-than-favorable opportunity. The same theory applies if your business is already established. By examining your financial position on a regular basis, you will be able to project how much you will need at a given point for expansion purposes. Always be aware.

7. ***Don't borrow if it is not necessary.*** Many businesses can be started for under $1,000. This is called "starting on a shoestring" and can be done with a variety of businesses. Services, for example, often rely strictly on the owner's knowledge and expertise and can be set up quickly and inexpensively.

 If this is the case with the business you have in mind, then try to avoid borrowing money, which can be an expensive and timely proposition.

Establishing Credit

Is it possible to get a loan even if you have never established credit? Yes, it is. If you prefer to pay cash rather than incur high interest charges on loans or credit cards, you can still qualify for a loan based on personal assets or by having a friend or relative with a good credit rating cosign for you on the loan. This puts the obligation on the cosigner, so be sure the terms of the loan are clearly spelled out in a written agreement to the satisfaction of everyone involved.

But, if your personal assets are minimal and you cannot find a cosigner, your best bet is to put off starting the business for four to six months while you establish credit. The best place to start is with a major department store. A store will issue you a credit card

based on a very simple examination of your income and employment history. When you receive the card, charge about $100 worth of merchandise and pay it off according to the schedule provided. Within a few months, you will have proven yourself to be creditworthy, which will greatly improve your chances of getting a loan from a lending institution.

Another way to establish credit—and credibility—is to open a checking account at the bank you have decided to approach for a loan. Banks generally require a minimum deposit of between $50 and $100. Make it a point to meet the branch manager and/or the loan officer and establish an ongoing relationship with them by stopping by to say hello when you are in the bank.

Within a few months, apply for a small personal loan, working with your new acquaintance, of course. Make your payments according to the prearranged schedule. Then when you are ready to request a more substantial amount of money to cover your start-up expenses, you will be recognized as a customer with a loan history at that institution.

Notes

Key Points

Personal Thoughts

Additional Research

14

RECORD KEEPING: YOUR BUSINESS LIFELINE

The motivating factor in any business is profit, which can be explained as the money left over after all the bills—everything from supplies to rent to salaries to taxes—are paid.

Building a profitable business is not something that can be left to chance; it must be planned, and a systematic method of record keeping must be developed to help you monitor income and expenses.

You should expect that during the early days of your business, your profits are going to be minimal as you become established. But it is possible, with even simple record-keeping procedures, to prepare yourself for lean periods and control day-to-day expenses to ensure that you are, at least, breaking even. In addition, financial records are required for tax purposes, and dealing with them systematically can help you avoid an incredibly overwhelming task at tax time.

Record Keeping Can Be Simple

Some people cringe at the thought of record keeping or feel it is a waste of valuable time. Usually, these attitudes are based on a lack

of knowledge and the feeling that it is a difficult job. There is, however, no other way to analyze your cash flow and make sure you are pricing products or services high enough to realize a profit.

In truth, record keeping is not a complicated process. If you have ever balanced a checkbook or planned a household budget, you have performed several of the same steps that are necessary for implementing a bookkeeping system for your business. And the good news is that keeping business records does not have to be either complicated or time consuming.

We know of entrepreneurs who opt for total simplicity by using the "shoe box" method—every sales record, receipt for expenses, and bank statement gets tossed into a box. This system has two distinct drawbacks. One may not become apparent until tax time, when you attempt to wade through and organize each sheet of paper to prepare your tax return. The other, more critical drawback is that it is virtually impossible to maintain an accurate picture of your financial situation when you stockpile, rather than record, business transactions.

In order to understand your cash flow, it is important to be able to see monies earned, monies paid out, current balances, and outstanding debts.

In fact, you should be able to answer the following questions with just a quick review of your records.

- ◆ What was my income last year (week, month)?
- ◆ What were my expenses?
- ◆ How do income and expenses compare with last year (week, month)?
- ◆ What was my profit (loss) last year (week, month)?
- ◆ Where can I cut back on expenses?
- ◆ Who and how much do I currently owe on outstanding debts?
- ◆ Who owes me money and how much?
- ◆ What are my assets, liabilities, and net worth?
- ◆ Is my inventory in line with demand?

◆ How much cash do I have available? How much credit?

◆ Am I able to pay myself this month (week)?

◆ Are my figures in line with projected financial goals?

The records you need to be able to answer most of these questions are your cash journal, a balance sheet, and a bank reconciliation. A simple single-entry system, as indicated on the following pages, where you can record disbursements (cash paid out) and receipts (cash taken in) will form the base of your record-keeping system.

*If you can organize your kitchen,
you can organize your life.*

Dr. Louis Parrish

Double-Entry Bookkeeping

You may want to consider a double-entry system, which involves recording each transaction twice; once as a debit (simply the left column of the ledger) and once as a credit (the right column of the ledger). For example, if you were to sell a product for $100, the transactions recorded in a double-entry system would be as follows: The $100 would be written as a *credit* in your sales account, since merchandise is going out of the business, and $100 would be recorded as a *debit* in your cash account since money was coming into the business.

This is a complex and time-consuming process that is often best left to an accountant, as he or she will need the information to create a monthly trial balance and other financial statements, including your year-end tax reports.

Bookkeeping Debits and Credits

Debits

- ◆ Cash receipts
- ◆ Purchases
- ◆ Expenses, such as rent and wages

Credits

- ◆ Cash payments
- ◆ Sales of services or merchandise
- ◆ Earnings, including interest

Single-Entry Bookkeeping

You can, however, set up a simple single-entry system, which will tie in directly with your accountant's requirements, or check out the standardized bookkeeping systems available at office supply or stationery stores, which provide all the necessary forms and documents in a bound book.

A system should contain forms for recording monthly income and expenses, summary sheets from which you can create a balance sheet, and listings of legal deductions for income tax reporting. In addition, the trade association for your field should be able to provide you with systems developed exclusively for use in the industry, which you can use or adapt according to the specific circumstances of your business.

The final method is to purchase a cash journal book and set up your own monthly system. (We've used Office Assistance, a small secretarial service that has been in operation for one month, as an example.) Any of the above-mentioned methods are acceptable, as long as you understand the entry process and can read the results.

Make Record Keeping a Daily Task

Short of paying someone else, the easiest way to be sure your records are kept up to date is to incorporate the task into your daily or weekly routine. Many small business owners make it a habit to enter their sales, expenses, and other financial information at the end of each working day. It keeps them continually aware of their financial situation and ensures that there will never be any cash-flow surprises.

The process shouldn't take more than fifteen minutes for normal transactions, and it will save hours of pencil pushing and frustration down the line. What's important is that you'll always know where you stand financially.

Setting Up the Books

Now, using Office Assistance, we will examine the various elements required for basic record-keeping duties.

Office Assistance has been in business for one month. Two months ago, Bill Miller, president of Office Assistance, opened a new business bank account with $10,000.00, his start-up capital from a personal savings account.

At the same time, he rented a small office in a downtown building for $350.00 a month, but had to pay the first month's rent, and a deposit of the last month's rent, for a total outlay of $700.00.

His fictitious name statement, which he got approved through the local county clerk's office, cost $10.00, and publishing it in a regional newspaper cost $45.00.

The initial month's lease and a deposit on a computer cost him $275.00, plus $50.00 for a maintenance agreement. However, he will own the $2,000.00 computer when his payment schedule is completed.

He found a brand-new calculator at a garage sale for $25.00 and is going to use a desk, table, lamp, and chairs brought from home (value $350.00) to decorate the office. Phone-line installation was $150.00, and he purchased a two-line telephone for $79.50.

An artist friend designed his logo and letterhead on a computer for only $25.00 and a $6.95 lunch. He had his stationery ($35.00), business cards ($60.00), and brochures ($23.50) produced through a local copy shop for a total of $118.50.

A 2 × 2-inch display ad in the local newspaper will cost him $370.00 for a week, and he is planning to mail 100 of his brochures to local businesses selected from the phone book. Stamps will cost $29.00 for the mailing. Office supplies, including typing paper, staples, paper clips, etc., set him back $45.00. A journal for record keeping cost $7.95 and a packet of invoices $5.95, for a grand total of $58.90.

Since he doesn't know how to type, Bill hired his niece to work 20 hours a week for $10.00 per hour on an independent contractor basis so he doesn't have to pay social security or unemployment taxes.

During the first month, he has billed and been paid $700.00. However, he has two clients who still owe him a total of $400.00. Bill dutifully records information in his cash journal at the end of each working day. He uses source documents, including his checkbook register, receipts from cash purchases, and billing invoices as the basis for his entries. The following cash journal illustrations are for May (prior to opening the doors of his business) and June (his first actual month in business).

Bill's expenses for May and June were $3,108.75. Of course, part of that is for start-up expenses, such as deposits on his rent and computer, installation costs, and one-time fictitious name filing and publishing. His income for the first month was $700.00.

Office Assistance
Cash Journal for May

Date	Check or Invoice #	Detail	(Debit) Expense	(Credit) Income
5/1	100	Rawlins Real Estate (rent & dep)	$700.00	
5/5	101	County Clerk (fictitious name)	10.00	
5/7	102	The Herald (publishing FNS)	45.00	
5/9	103	Ed's Keyboards (IBM 1-mo. & dep)	275.00	
5/9	104	Ed's Keyboards (maint. agreement)	50.00	
5/12	105	Mary Smith (calculator purchase)	25.00	
5/18	106	Telephone Co. (line installation)	150.00	
5/20	107	Phone Store (2-line phone)	79.50	
5/22	108	Ray Brown (logo design)	25.00	
5/24	Cash	The Hungry Dog (lunch/Ray Brown)	6.95	
5/28	109	The Copy Spot (brochures, cards)	118.50	
5/29	110	The Herald (advertising)	370.00	
		Total Expense & Income (May)	**$1,854.95**	**$00.00**

Office Assistance
Cash Journal for June

Date	Check or Invoice #	Detail	(Debit) Expense	(Credit) Income
6/4	111	U.S.P.O. (stamps for mailing)	$29.00	
6/6	112	Office Stationers (supplies, invoices, etc.)	58.90	
6/7	A1	W. Smith		$62.50
6/8	A2	Art Association		112.50
6/9	A3	T. Williams		22.00
6/9	113	Judy Miller (typing fee)	200.00	
6/10	A4	Bank of Cutterville		75.00
6/10	A5	WKTR-FM		120.50
6/13	A6	J. Johnson		43.50
6/15	114	Rawlins Real Estate (rent)	350.00	
6/15	A7	C. Lewis		73.50
6/15	A8	R. Swell		90.00
6/16	115	Judy Miller (typing fee)	200.00	
6/19	A9	W. Smith		52.50
6/23	116	Judy Miller (typing fee)	200.00	
6/26	117	Phone company (bill)	15.90	
6/27	A10	K. Black		48.00
6/30	118	Judy Miller (typing fee)	200.00	
		Total Expense & Income (June)	**$1,253.80**	**$700.00**

By deducting his expenses from his income, he can see that, at the moment, his business is showing a loss of $2,408.75.

Although Bill has only been in business for a month, he is curious about his company's financial worth and decides to work up a balance sheet to get the answer. The calculation, as indicated in the example, is the amount owned (assets) minus the amount due to creditors (liabilities), which equals his worth.

Balance Sheet (as of June 30)

Assets		Liabilities	
Cash on hand & in bank	$6,191.25	Ed's Keyboards	$1,725.00
(Capital balance &		*(Balance on IBM)*	
June Income)		Unpaid rent *(July)*	350.00
Office equipment	2,000.00	Taxes *(estimated)*	75.00
(Includes full value			
of IBM even though			
not paid off)			
Office furniture	350.00	**Liabilities**	**$2,150.00**
Accounts receivable			
(outstanding invoices			
for work already done)	400.00		
Total Assets	**$8,941.25**	**CAPITAL**	**$6,791.25**
		Total Liabilities	**$8,941.25**

The figure Bill is most interested in is the CAPITAL amount in the Liabilities column. This is the amount remaining after what Bill owes is subtracted from his current assets and is what his business is worth at the end of June. In other words, if he decided to try to sell his business right now, he could realistically ask that amount as a selling price. Of course, Bill probably wouldn't get that amount because he has not yet become established enough to warrant someone buying the business, unless he or she was looking for a "turnkey" operation—in other words, a business to just walk into and get going immediately.

This information is valuable when Bill goes to apply for expansion capital or for credit on future purchases he plans to make. His balance sheet will change each time he prepares it (probably quarterly in the future) as business improves, bringing in greater income and reducing his debts.

In the meantime, the balance sheet gives Bill a tool to use when comparing the financial standing of his business this month against future months and years. It also keeps him current on what he owns, to whom he owes money, and his major sources of income.

The same procedure is used in developing a personal balance sheet, which possibly would be needed to establish credibility when applying for a loan. Assets would include furniture, automobiles, jewelry, a home, and other tangibles, while liabilities would consist of outstanding loans and other major debts.

Bank Statement Reconciliation

Another important step that Bill must handle monthly is reconciling his bank statement against his checkbook register. He simply marks off the checks in his register that have cleared per the bank statement, notes the deposits that have been credited, and deducts any service charges for the previous month from his balance.

Bill then adds up all the outstanding checks—those listed in his register that have not cleared by the closing date indicated on the bank statement—and *deducts* them from the balance indicated on his bank statement. He adds up any deposits that have not yet been credited to his account and then *adds* them to the balance, as follows.

Balance per bank statement	$5,982.15
Plus: Deposits not credited	+325.00
Minus: Outstanding checks	-115.90
New Balance	$6,191.25

The new balance figure should match that listed in his checkbook register and, in this case, it does. If, however, the statement and

the register did not reconcile, Bill would have a customer representative at the bank review his statement and banking activity for the past month.

A Simplified System for Charting Orders

It's absolutely crucial that you keep good records. How you accomplish this can range from performing the job yourself to using an accountant, if the size of your business dictates it. Because you're most likely starting small and at home, we'll focus on the basic methods.

A simple record-keeping system will allow you to track all the information you need on one chart. Take a three-ring binder and fill it with blank paper. On one sheet draw twelve horizontal lines. Across the top, make the following headings: date order received, name of customer, address of customer, amount enclosed, inquiry, method of payment, date order filled, postage cost, key code.

These headings allows you to record important information:

1. *Date order received.* Important for two reasons: follow-up in the case of fulfillment delays or customer complaints and for tax purposes.

2. *Name of customer.* Aside from the obvious importance here, remember that you want to follow up with your customers, and that later you can make money selling your valuable mailing list to other mail order companies. When you enter this information on your sheet, fill out a file card or enter the data into your computer.

3. *Address of customer.* Always double-check to make sure you have the right address. Having it in two places (on the sheet and on a file card) lets you check one against the other. Be sure to use ZIP codes.

4. *Amount enclosed.* This is where you see how much money you're making in mail order. At a glance, you can tell how things are going.

5. *Inquiry.* This is when the customer has sent no money and just wants information. Use this information to see

how specific ads pull orders vs. inquiries, then see how you convert follow-ups to sales.

6. ***Method of payment.*** Tracks cash, check, money order, or credit card.

7. ***Date order filled.*** This date is important in that it verifies each order has been mailed.

8. ***Postage cost.*** For frame of reference and tax purposes, you'll want to know how much you're spending on postage each month.

9. ***Key code.*** Lets you know which ads are working best for you.

You'll also need to keep files for correspondence, advertising and business expense, and tax records. You can use the method described earlier for business expenses by heading the top of the paper with: date expense incurred, description, advertising expense, printing expense, professional service expense.

As your business grows, you'll need to adjust your record-keeping system accordingly, and there may come a point where the simple methods described here no longer work for you. As the need arises, do some research at the local library about basic accounting methods.

Remember: *The most important thing is that you keep records that are clear to you and that substantiate expenses for income tax purposes.*

15

PRICING FOR PROFITS

One of the toughest problems facing small business owners is establishing prices that the market will bear and that will cover overhead and guarantee a profit.

Often new business owners give the business away to get sales, but this is not an advisable practice. Realistic pricing indicates your confidence in what you are selling, and if you value your service, so will the customer.

Today's consumer realizes that no one gets something worthwhile for nothing, so don't be afraid to establish prices that will work toward your profit goals.

Mail Order Pricing Is Unique

You're probably most familiar with prices you encounter while retail shopping. This system is based on a formula of a percentage markup over cost to include overhead and profit. Mail order pricing is an entirely different approach, one that is more concerned with psychology than economics. In mail order, you want to charge approximately the maximum amount most people are willing to pay, without reference to actual cost.

Unlike the retailer, you don't need to be concerned with such things as cost, overhead, and profit to retailer, distributor, wholesaler and manufacturer—all of whom must also take care of taxes, wages, salaries, insurance, and so on.

The important thing to consider in setting a price for your products or services is to find a balance between how much you're selling and how much you're earning. You want to make as much money as you can while offering a good product at a fair price. Your customers will let you know whether that price is fair. This means that, even though it only costs you $3 to make a pair of earrings, if most of your customers are willing to pay $10 a pair, you should charge $10 a pair.

Higher Profit Margin

It's easy to see how much rosier the profit picture is for a mail order operator compared to retailers. If you sold those same earrings for $10 through standard retail methods, you might be lucky to see $1 profit. By eliminating all of the middlemen—you are the distributor and, if you produce what you sell, the manufacturer—you can afford more flexibility in your pricing.

If you see earrings like yours selling in stores for $10, you can offer them at $7—getting advertising mileage because your prices are less than in a retail location—and still turn a tidy profit. Just be sure that you always leave yourself a comfortable margin between cost plus overhead and profits.

You're going into this business to make money, plain and simple. Never let your expenses threaten your proceeds. If they do, go back to square one and start again.

Another factor to consider in setting prices is the uniqueness of your product. Customers not only want to pay less for something than they would locally, but they also want a product or service that is, in some way different. This will take some effort on your part, mostly in the way of research. Find out what's out there. Let's say you find three different suppliers who sell earrings similar to yours. You'll want yours to come in different colors or made from more unique materials.

Experience shows that most customers buy mail order goods priced in whole dollar amounts. They will also generally make a

purchase of up to $5 simply by reading about the product in a classified ad. Items priced over $5 will often require a direct mail follow-up, which will be discussed in Chapter 20. Most products priced over $10 don't do well unless they are offered by a recognized leader in the business, are unique, or targeted to a specific market.

The bottom line is profits. To maximize your potential you must price products with a strict line on your cost plus overhead profile. Make sure you pay the best price possible for your product or raw materials (taking into account any discounts or price breaks for quantity); keep your overhead expenses low by hunting for the best prices in packaging materials, printing of promotional pieces, and finding good advertising values; and make sure to charge what the market is willing to pay.

Guidelines

Several factors must be taken into consideration when setting prices:

1. *The cost of goods sold.* In the case of a retail or wholesale operation, this is the amount originally paid for the goods. For a manufacturer, it is the cost of producing the goods.

2. *The nature of the product or service.* Uniqueness and demand come into play here. In the case of goods with a stable level of demand, such as bread or auto repair, raising or lowering prices will have little effect. However, when demand is high for goods that are hard to get, the price can realistically be set anywhere the business owner wants. Such is often the case with restaurants featuring an exclusive or unusual menu.

3. *The competition.* It is important to recognize what your competition is charging, for often this will guide pricing within a certain region. However, if a competitor is charging what you feel is an unrealistic price—either more or less—for a product or service, you owe it to yourself to find out why. Then set your prices according to all of the

factors outlined here. Even if your prices are higher than the competitor, consumers will pay the cost if you offer something special, such as a friendly atmosphere, convenient hours, follow-up service or maintenance, or some other benefit not provided by the competition.

4. ***Your company policy.*** This encompasses a number of things, including your location, your position in the marketplace, and additional services offered. It also takes into account your personal philosophy about business and your role in it.

5. ***Market strategy.*** Should you go for large volume at low prices or for low volume at high prices? That is the bottom line in considering market strategy. As a small business owner, you will likely opt for low volume and higher prices, since the alternative involves having the resources, including labor, display room, distribution channels, etc., to move large volumes of product or perform major service tasks.

6. ***Customers.*** What will the market bear? In other words, what are your customers willing to pay for your products or services?

People expect prices that are fair; if you are planning to charge overinflated rates you had better be a topnotch salesperson or have something so incredible and unusual to offer that the price won't matter.

Although there are differences between establishing prices for retail operations, wholesale products, manufacturing, and services, the basic formula for price setting is

Labor + Materials + Overhead + Profit Margin = Price

However, before setting prices on goods or services, it is extremely important to understand the concept of the break-even point. Many small business owners operate on an overall profit-loss basis without realizing the importance of cost accounting. Being aware

of such factors as your break-even point, markup, and profit margin can tell you which areas of your business are profitable and which are causing a drain.

Understanding Break-even

The break-even point is the minimum amount you must charge in order to cover all expenses incurred for the production and promotion of your goods and/or services *without losing or making money.* In other words, any income that is above the break-even point is considered to be profit and anything below it is a loss.

To find your break-even point, you must first total all of your operating costs, including materials and labor, equipment lease or purchase payments, advertising, utilities, office supplies, and any incidentals such as gasoline, maintenance, and postage.

Generally, this is computed for a particular period of time, such as six months or a year. However, if your business is still in the early stages of operation, you can use the estimated figures on your projected expenses statement and guesstimate costs for materials and labor.

For example, the monthly expenses for your hypothetical cake-decorating business total $300.00. You want to know what the break-even point would be if you sold an average of 20 cakes per month. The calculation is as follows:

$$\frac{\$300.00 \text{ (expenses)}}{20 \text{ cakes}} = \$15.00$$

In order to break even, that is, to operate without losing money or realizing a profit, you must charge a minimum of $15.00 for each cake sold.

The same process can be used to analyze the break-even point on a weekly basis. First you determine your annual expenses by multiplying the $300.00 by 12 months, which would give you $3,600.00 per year.

The calculation to find the weekly break-even point follows:

$$\frac{\$3,600.00 \text{ (expenses)}}{52 \text{ weeks}} = \$69.23$$

Therefore, you must earn $69.23 per week to operate the business without losing money and without realizing a profit.

Stay Informed

Knowing your break-even point is one of the greatest favors you can do for yourself as a business owner. It tells you how much you must charge for your products or services and is invaluable in setting prices to realize a profit.

Keep in mind, however, that the break-even point is a variable figure. Since it depends on production and overhead costs, plan to reevaluate periodically to make sure your prices reflect any changes.

Labor Costs

Labor costs, obviously, are the expenses incurred for the actual work done to manufacture or sell a product or to perform a service. Think of them as wages or salaries.

Small business owners often end up working for free because they fail to set a wage for themselves. Despite the fact that you will want to reinvest all of the income received back into the business for a while, it is imperative that you establish a fixed salary amount for yourself when figuring operating expenses.

If you have set aside a survival fund to carry you through the first six months of operation, you may want to defer your salary until the business becomes solvent; however, you should still figure the amount into your expenses. Otherwise, you may find the prices you set are too low to justify making a profit from the onset.

It is much easier to set realistic prices from the beginning than it is to raise them later in an attempt to make up the difference. Remember, your time and skills are the cornerstone of your

business, so think of paying yourself as you would any valuable employee.

And remember, the most important variables to take into account when developing a price structure are

1. Your costs
2. Your expected profit

Notes

Key Points

Personal Thoughts

Additional Research

16

INVENTORY AS INVESTMENT

Ask 100 small business owners what inventory means to them and more than 90 percent will tell you it's the merchandise they keep on hand to sell to their customers, or the materials and supplies stocked to produce goods or perform a service.

This is somewhat accurate, for inventory can and should be viewed as any supplies, raw materials, or finished goods used to generate a profit in your business. But it isn't the response that a savvy business owner would give.

Surprisingly, according to a recent study conducted by a leading consulting firm, less than 10 percent of a group of 500 entrepreneurs interviewed spoke of their inventory in terms of the *investment it represents;* an investment that can range from 15 to 25 percent of total operating capital.

It is because of this misunderstanding that many small business owners often fail to incorporate good inventory control practices into their regular management routine. Although they keep an eagle eye on every penny going through the books, they may totally overlook the cash tied up in their inventory.

Controlling Inventory

Inventory control can be a very simple, straightforward task if you implement a workable system from the beginning—preferably even *before* you start ordering and receiving goods. You will find that time really flies when you are self-employed, and it's very easy to postpone such tasks as inventory control until the inevitable day you find yourself facing this overwhelming job. Inventory control will give you valuable information about: (a) whether or not you are carrying too much or too little inventory based on, for example, items and prices preferred by your customers, or seasonal aspects, and (b) if you are realizing optimum economy determined by the costs of storage, taxes, handling, and the investment per unit.

The ideal situation is to maintain an inventory that is profitable because it turns over (comes in and goes out of the business) regularly, thereby lowering the cost of storing, displaying, and insuring it.

Although there are countless alumni of the school of hard knocks, there has not yet been a move to accredit that institution.

Sonya Rudikoff

There are several methods of inventory control that you can adopt, depending on your business. The main goal with each method, however, is to tell you how many items you have on hand and how many you need to meet your customer or production demands. It will also work toward lessening inventory shrinkage, which is generally the result of employee pilferage; customer theft; incorrect inventory storage; or sloppy record maintenance of items ordered, received, and used.

You can tell how many items you currently have by making an educated guess, which generally only works for businesses having a small, visible inventory that is relatively predictable. An example of the kind the business that could probably operate efficiently with this relaxed form of inventory control would be a

one- or two-person enterprise that monthly goes through a box of invoices and similar supplies available for a minimum amount at the discount office-supply store.

Other methods of inventory control are *the physical count,* which should be done at least once a year for tax purposes, or–the easiest and most efficient of them all–*an ongoing* record. Ideally, you should incorporate both systems by backing up periodic physical counts with a perpetual record.

To set up your perpetual system, simply create a file card or inventory sheet in a three-ring binder for each item in your inventory. Across the top of the card or sheet, list the following:

1. Item name and code number, if applicable

2. A description of the item

3. Where it is stored

4. The supplier's name, address, and phone number

5. Unit price (i.e., $12.95/dozen)

6. Your selling price if a retail item, or percentage of gross price of completed product, if used for manufacturing or service

7. The date you place an order

8. The number of items and the date they are received

Then, every time you sell or use an item, write it down and subtract it from the last balance. You should also indicate the reorder number, based on when and by how much you must replenish your stock.

The reorder number will be determined by such factors as the following:

1. The minimum cost per unit available from your supplier, including quantity discounts, preseason specials, and discounts for cash or quick payment

2. The delivery schedule–the delay between placing the order and receiving it

3. Economic and social trends that can affect the way an item is perceived by the public

For example, during a depressed or inflated economy, sales for leisure items typically drop. By keeping an eye on these factors, you can adjust your inventory needs accordingly and not get stuck with great quantities of items that you can't move.

After a while, you will be able to recognize at a glance which items are movers and which are simply taking up shelf space. When you reach this point, your ordering skills will become much more efficient and your investment in inventory will become a profitable proposition.

Notes

Key Points

Personal Thoughts

Additional Research

17

MAKING THE MOST OF YOUR TIME

A recent survey of small business owners indicated that one of the qualities they felt contributed the most to their success was organization. In conjunction with this is the fact that time management and basic organizational seminars continue to be the most popular offerings in adult education catalogs and business workshops around the country.

Time is money! It is vital to your success that you learn to manage your time and organize paperwork. This might sound rather simplistic, but you would be amazed at the number of small business owners who operate in a constant state of chaos.

Although we have seen a number of "A messy office is the sign of a creative mind" posters on entrepreneurs' office walls, it is a good bet that the holders of these signs can recount story after story of missing checks, lost orders, or misplaced files, which disrupted or halted the flow of business until they were located.

The survey respondents also stated that once they had learned to manage their time in both their personal and business lives and had set up guidelines for handling routine tasks, they felt more confident about accepting new challenges and making decisions.

The simple truth about getting organized is that it clears your mind for taking care of the nitty-gritty, profit-making aspects of being in business—production and promotion. For example, just by setting aside a certain place in your work area to hold customer files and billing information, you have made one major step toward maximizing production. Knowing that all the supplies and materials needed to conduct your business are located in one place saves you both time and energy.

Making Time Work for You

Time management is the ability to take the hours we have available and use them to our advantage. Making lists of tasks to be done and giving them a priority rating is one of the best ways to avoid losing precious moments.

Keep a monthly calendar handy to help you keep track of major commitments, important dates, and appointments. Try to avoid using it for notations of daily work in progress, carryover tasks, or other things that are best suited for inclusion on your daily and weekly lists. There are several other ideas you can easily incorporate into your working lifestyle that will maximize your productivity.

Work Smart

Handle the jobs you find most difficult or cumbersome during peak performance time. If you are a morning person and find that making telephone calls to potential customers is one of your least favorite tasks, make those calls first thing in the morning when you are feeling fresh and energetic. Then organize the rest of the day's tasks accordingly.

Set Realistic Daily Goals for Yourself

Just because you are the key employee, don't try to do everything at once. Learn just how much work you can accept and expect to accomplish in a given period of time and allow yourself to turn down work if it seems like it will be too much for you to handle.

Positive Reinforcement

When you work alone, as many small business owners do when getting their businesses off the ground, there generally aren't many people around to support or praise your work...and everyone needs strokes! Remember that a customer's praises are proof that you are doing a good job.

Reward Yourself

Sometimes it is easy to forget that you are important to the business—you *are* the business. So treat yourself to a special dinner now and then or plan an evening where you go out to a movie or do something else that has absolutely nothing to do with business. Remind yourself that this is your reward for accomplishing certain goals for your business. It will help to keep your spirits high.

Don't Procrastinate

Don't put off doing tasks that must be done. If you constantly let some tasks slide because you don't enjoy doing them or they are boring and time-consuming, you will soon find yourself back-logged and unable to catch up. The effects of procrastination may not be obvious until you are faced with a deadline and, at that point, you will realize that you are working at less than maximum efficiency using the wrong supplies, feeling tense, and being hassled by minor problems that could have been avoided. Even when business is slow and it seems that there could be little harm done by taking a day off to go to the beach, be sure to complete all your required tasks before closing up shop.

Limit Personal Phone Calls

Ask friends and relatives not to call during established business hours. These friendly calls not only eat into productive time, they tie up the line when an important client may be trying to get in touch with you. The same holds true with visitors. If you are self-employed, friends and family often feel that you are not really "working" and that they can stop by anytime to chat. Explain that you will be happy to visit with them at some other time and be sure to tell them why so there aren't any ill feelings.

Obviously, there will be times when unavoidable situations arise, such as an emergency or an unexpected problem. Take these into consideration by estimating how long a project will take and then adding a bit of extra time to give yourself some leeway.

Delegate

If you find that you absolutely cannot handle a certain aspect of the business, such as your own bookkeeping, for example, don't labor over the task—you will end up wasting a great deal of time and could make some serious mistakes. Admit to yourself that the task is just not your strong point and make arrangements to have someone else do it.

Learn to Say "No"

One of the hardest things for most people to do is to say "no." Even when we realize that helping a friend out on a special project will cost valuable time, we often agree to do it because we hate to say no. What we do is justify our acceptance by assuring ourselves that saying yes will put us in the position of meeting a lot of potential customers. The reality is that using that time to make phone calls or a sales call for your own business will probably result in a paying customer, not just a potential contact.

Minimize Business Meetings

Before setting up a formal meeting, which can be very time consuming, see if you can take care of the matter by phone or through the mail. If a meeting can't be avoided, make sure you specify a time limit to encourage people to get down to business. Another time-saving device for meetings is to work up an agenda that outlines exactly what has to be discussed to avoid idle chit-chat and unnecessary diversions.

Plan Your Time

When you have to run errands, plan them for a sensible time, such as in the morning when traffic is light. Plan to do as many things as possible in one trip, outlining the stops you must make so they follow a sequential order.

Notes

Key Points

Personal Thoughts

Additional Research

18

GETTING DOWN TO BUSINESS

You've made your decision and now it's time to start the business, but there are still a number of steps to accomplish before you mail out that first package. At this point, it's a good idea to map out a general plan of action that starts at Step One and continues to that first fulfilled order.

1. Choose your product or service.
2. Choose your company name and obtain a post office box.
3. Locate suppliers and get prices; find out about availability and lead time for ordering.
4. Locate a printer and have stationery and business forms printed.
5. Set up your office and filing system.
6. Prepare your tentative classified advertisements.
7. Select the media and place ads through a representative.
8. Prepare your direct-mail materials.
9. Secure a reply mail permit if desired.
10. Order printing of follow-up direct-mail materials.
11. Prepare and stuff a quantity of reply materials.

12. Stock inventory.

13. As orders/responses come in from ads, track response levels per key codes.

14. _____?

This is a linear flow of how things should basically progress as you get the business started. We'll get to more specifics shortly, but for the moment, let's get back to that question mark indicated in number 14 and take a general look at what happens after the first responses have been received and looked at.

Your First Mailing

The results of your initial assault will either encourage you or discourage you. If the numbers look good, you're doing something right and should proceed accordingly. If they don't look so good, however, you may still be doing something right, which is to say you shouldn't despair if your first effort doesn't reward you like you thought it would. Whatever the response, your reward is information, and that's the basic function of your first mailing.

To maintain momentum in your business, you need to continually evaluate how well your product or service sells, then build your advertising program based on what works, plain and simple. You'll need to set reasonable sales goals for the first three months.

The greater the difficulty, the more glory there is in surmounting it. Skillful pilots gain their reputation from storms and tempests.

Anonymous

If those goals are not attained within reason, you must reevaluate what it is you're selling. Any time is a good time to look around for something new to test. If you tested a product you've manufactured without favorable results, try someone else's product.

And if your first product does well, at some point you may want to add another.

Finding Viable Products

There are various ways that you can find products. Attend trade shows and expositions, where hundreds of manufacturers gather to display and sell new products. You may spend hours following up on leads from friends or looking at classified ads in the Business Opportunities section of the newspaper. Then there are the potential profit makers discovered through manufacturer's showrooms and Inventors' Clubs (if one exists in your area).

You also may find clues to a unique item by visiting galleries and studios of local artists and crafts people. Even though an artisan may not be able to handle mass production, he or she may be willing to sell you an original design or give you the exclusive rights to manufacture, promote, and sell copies of a creation.

Mail Order Tip

Always test a product before investing a lot of time and money on mass marketing. Run one ad in a publication that attracts other mail order distributors to reach a general mail order audience, or place an ad in a specialty publication that is geared to the kind of shopper you want to attract.

Other Resources

It is in your best interest to subscribe to magazines and newsletters geared to the type of products you are interested in selling. These are known as trade publications. Not only will you learn a great deal from the articles in them, you will also find a wealth of prospective merchandise through the advertisements placed by both manufacturers and retailers.

Check with your local library for the pertinent copy of the *Standard Rate & Data Service* reference to find names and

addresses of appropriate publications. Another source for names is *Bacon's Publicity Checker,* under the Mail Order Industry market classification.

Get your hands on as many mail order catalogs as possible. Study them thoroughly to get an idea of current offerings. You will also find them an invaluable source of information and ideas when you plan advertising. The library should have a copy of the *U.S. Mail Order Shoppers Guide,* which provides a concise listing of available catalogs. Or you can purchase a directory of catalogs from the Direct Marketing Association. For information, contact:

> Direct Marketing Association, Inc.
> 11 West 42nd Street, 25th Floor
> New York, NY, 10036

Be sure to tell everyone you know that you are always in the market for products with mail order potential. Or consider running an ad in the local classified section. For example:

> TREASURE HUNT!!
> Seeking Mail Order Products
> Call Bill at 555-1111

The continual profitable building of your business requires that your products have the following characteristics:

- ♦ Practicality—buyer *needs* item OR
- ♦ Originality—buyer *wants* item OR BOTH
- ♦ Fair and honest pricing
- ♦ Easy to pack and ship
- ♦ Durable construction, no breakable parts
- ♦ Lightweight to keep postage costs down
- ♦ Inventory required is minimal
- ♦ Maintains steady profits over cost-plus-overhead

By the way: Your customers will let you know how you're doing. Mail order buyers can be a very responsive group, so pay attention to the feedback you get. What better source of knowledge about the quality of your business than your consumers?

If you want to make money, go where the money is.
Joseph P. Kennedy

And Speaking of Your Customers...

Success in your mail order venture is largely dependent on *customer service.* One of the first things you need to get a feel for—and to maintain an awareness of—is what your customers desire in the way of products or services. We talked a little earlier about who your customers are. Now let's talk about what they want.

There are a number of basic assumptions you can make about mail order customers, characteristics that have been determined through market research conducted by big-name advertising companies.

1. They have money and are willing to buy something they think will be a pleasure to own, is of good quality, and comes at the right price.

2. They are experienced mail order shoppers, and their experiences have generally been good.

3. They will read your advertisements if you catch their attention.

4. They will wait two to three weeks for an order without concern. If it takes longer, they will probably not be repeat customers, unless you maintain ongoing communication with them about the status of their order.

5. They are much more likely to respond to ads offering something for free, even if all that's being offered is advertising or sales information.

6. They are less likely to respond if they are required to enclose stamps or coins for postage and handling. Many mail order companies build in the costs of shipping and handling into the unit price.

7. They generally have unreadable handwriting–ask them to type or print their names and addresses.

8. They like language that makes them feel like they're getting a great deal. Words and phrases like *free, bonus, premium, guaranteed, money back if not satisfied, orders shipped in 24 hours, sale, closeout prices,* and so on, will always work for you. (One point to remember: There are legal considerations that must be observed.)

9. They don't like to work at understanding what you're trying to say. Keep your ads simple enough for a fourth grader to understand.

10. They don't trust overly fancy advertisements and will take offense at high-pressure tactics.

11. They can smell something fishy a mile away.

12. They are mostly honest–very few will write bad checks.

13. They are basically lazy and will not often go to the trouble to return merchandise they're not happy with. Putting a return package together and getting it off in the mail is more of a headache than most customers want. (Some mail order companies–record, tape, and book clubs, for example–further ensure a low return rate by designing their shipping cartons so that they must be destroyed to get the merchandise out!)

14. They are interested in learning about new things, so long as the information is accessible and doesn't require too much effort on their part.

One of the most important words in the operator-customer relationship is trust. You are dealing with people who trust you–if they didn't, they wouldn't send you their checks, money orders, or credit card numbers. They order your product knowing they won't

see their merchandise for up to four weeks, and knowing further they can't be *exactly* sure of what it is they ordered until it arrives.

What can you do to be sure that these people feel trusting enough to send you their orders, especially when you're new in the business? The best thing you can do is create advertising that points out your commitment to

- ♦ Quality products with attention to workmanship, material, and other manufacturing components
- ♦ Unique merchandise that is not found everywhere
- ♦ Fair pricing, but not so inexpensive as to make the potential buyer uneasy about the quality
- ♦ Simple ordering procedures and speedy delivery
- ♦ Prompt handling of all customer correspondence, and guaranteed satisfaction

It's very important to establish a personal touch and a sense of relationship with your customers. One way to achieve this is to send a photocopied note, written and signed by your company's customer service manager, with each order. Here's a sample:

Mary Smith's Trinkets 'N' Stuff
P.O. Box 111 Big Town, U.S.A.

Hi, there! I'm delighted you decided to place your order with Trinkets 'N' Stuff. Your merchandise is enclosed. All of us here in Big Town are pleased that we can add your name to our list of satisfied customers. I have enclosed a flyer describing several of our newest products, along with an order form for your convenience.

If you have any questions or comments, please feel free to drop me a line at the address above.

Sincerely,

Customer Service

P.S. Just wanted to remind you to look for our upcoming "Shop Early for Christmas" catalog, which should be in your mailbox soon!

Even if you run a one-person operation, you should come up with a person's name to use for customer correspondence. You'll be amazed at the number of letters your customer service manager (you) receives. Just be certain that, regardless of whether they are letters of praise or complaint, that each and every one is given a "personal" response to solidify your reputation of dependability.

As you grow in the mail order business, you'll learn more about what your customers want and need. And the more you learn, the more you'll earn.

The Matter of Ethics

On the flip side of your business management coin are the day-to-day chores, logistics, and operational considerations common to every small business owner. You'll make decisions about how to organize specific tasks such as paperwork and filing based on what works best for you; trial and error is the best teacher in these areas.

You need to be aware, though, of certain ethical responsibilities you have as the operator of a mail order business. Some of your management habits may be dictated by these responsibilities.

While there is no written code of ethics for the mail order industry, you should have your own personal code that determines how you do business. Because this is an industry where money is exchanged between strangers sight unseen, there is a certain amount of potential abuse. Most operators are honest, but those who are not damage the credibility of all mail order businesses. To keep yourself clear—because sometimes the lines are hazy—ask yourself every so often: Am I conducting a business that would make me happy if I were a customer? There's nothing like following the Golden Rule to keep one honest.

Hiring Employees

At some point down the road you may need some help in running the business. But until you are handling tremendous volume, you'll probably get by with help from your family or neighbors, paid for on an hourly basis.

Start with part-time employees who work on an as-needed basis. If possible, hire them as independent contractors, which

means they will take care of their own insurance and taxes. This saves you time and money.

Finding Qualified Staff

You can find employees through ads in the classified section of the newspaper, through listings with college employment offices, or by word of mouth to friends and relatives.

Have interested applicants fill out a standard employment application (available in any stationery store) and make sure they provide references from former employers. Check these references very carefully to find out about the applicant's sense of loyalty, responsibility, and honesty.

Schedule a personal interview to make your own determination based on personality, level of interest in the job, abilities, and future goals. Then add the recruit's name to your roster of employees to call when needed.

Notes

Key Points

Personal Thoughts

Additional Research

19

FIFTY MAIL ORDER SUCCESS TIPS

The following tips and hints compiled from mail order operators we interviewed for this book should help you keep in mind some important ideas as you follow the road to mail order success.

1. Use short, attractive sentences to hook prospects into reading your classified ads.

2. Try to acknowledge every order you receive. It's good business.

3. Be sure to use a professional-looking letterhead for all your business correspondence. Always type your letters.

4. Avoid pie-in-the-sky copy in your ads promising unbelievable or overnight products or services. Don't try to fool prospects. Offer genuine value for their money.

5. Watch for important trends in the industry.

6. Develop your creative and inventive abilities. This can lead to a jackpot.

7. Sell low-priced items directly from an ad for best results.

8. Guarantee your products and offers. You'll get more orders.

9. Avoid any offer that smacks of a chain letter or pyramid scheme.

10. Set a regular time for thinking up new product or service ideas for your business.

11. Offer a short manual on any subject—they often sell well.

12. Keep track of your growing customer list. An index card system is sufficient if you do not have a computer available.

13. Clip out classified and display ads that you feel are especially effective. Save them for future reference.

14. Allow for the rising postage rate in your direct mailings.

15. Use inquiry and follow-up classified ads for higher-priced offers.

16. Don't use a catalog, which is costly to produce, to sell what you have until your customer list has at least 10,000 names.

17. Always enclose a reply envelope—preferably a prepaid one.

18. One hundred dollars spent on a direct mailing to 1,000 names should return you $300 or more. Anything less is not profitable enough. Higher postage rates will call for adjustment of these figures in the years ahead.

19. Before you offer a new product or service, decide who your customers are and the best form of advertising to reach them.

20. Keep your eyes and ears open for profitable new business ideas.

21. Handle any complaints immediately. Respond with a courteous letter of explanation.

22. Use the extra incentive of a free bonus gift. It's a proven way to increase your orders.

23. Develop a short, easy-to-remember name for your mail order company.

24. Advertise consistently—it's the only way to make money in mail order.

25. Using a P.S.(postscript) at the end of your direct-mail sales letter gives your offer additional pulling power because of the personal, confidential connotation.

26. Remember that the names you receive from the requests for details on your offers can grow into a profitable mailing list.

27. Write the copy for your ads with the mass audience in mind.

28. Watch the ads in leading mail order publications. Request details yourself, so you can look over current offers and literature used to sell them.

29. Don't start a mail order company if you expect to make a fortune overnight. Figure on six months to two years to break even.

30. Try to get the quality of sincerity into your sales letters.

31. Start your mail order business with small classified ads.

32. Sign all your outgoing letters. It creates a good impression.

33. Write crisp, fresh copy for your ads. Make every word pull its weight.

34. Stick with a successful ad until the returns from it begin to fizzle out.

35. Use an order form built into your sales letter to save money.

36. Key every ad that you run.

37. Know at all times what your competition is offering.

38. Avoid selling heavy items, so the shipping expenses won't eat up your profits.

39. Keep a copy of every business letter you send out.

40. Realize that "five times as many people read a headline as read the body of an ad," according to David Ogilvy, the veteran advertising expert.

41. Send a refund at once to anyone who requests it.

42. Use color in your direct-mail package whenever possible.

43. Realize that most checks received with mail orders will be good.

44. Keep close tabs on the amount of stock you have on hand for each item. Avoid overstocking items that don't sell.

45. Follow up on those who send you requests for details on an offer. If they don't send an order right away, try again later. Inquiry names have been sold on the twentieth and thirtieth attempts, so don't be too quick to give up on them.

46. Quote your asking price in round dollars for low-priced items.

47. Offer new items from time to time to your growing customer list. Many will buy from you again and again.

48. Do your best to fill orders within twenty-four hours.

49. Start out with a low-priced item, but try to sell a higher priced offer as soon as possible. It will be more profitable.

50. STICK TO IT!!

Notes

Key Points

Personal Thoughts

Additional Research

20

ADVERTISING YOUR BUSINESS

More than 150 years ago, Thomas Macaulay, a British historian and statesman, said, "Advertising is to business what steam is to industry. [They provide] the same propelling power."

Few in business would argue with Macaulay's observation—it is as true today as it was when steam was the driving force behind industry. But the question remains, "How do you get the most out of your advertising dollar?" The answer is to

1. Know your customer
2. Target your market
3. Understand the basics of advertising

In this chapter, we will provide an overview of various aspects of advertising, including how to use circulation figures to figure your cost per thousand (CPM) and how to create ads that will bring results.

What Is Advertising?

Advertising informs the public about

◆ Who you are

◆ What kind of business you operate

◆ How they can buy your products or services

◆ Why they should come to you

Before you even open the doors of your business, you should start thinking about your advertising program—how much money you can afford to spend, where your dollars will be best spent, and how to structure your campaign.

Decide what kind of results you want. Are you looking for immediate sales or ongoing recognition? What kind of customers are you hoping to attract? Are you emphasizing price, service, workmanship, or something unique? Once you have answered these questions, your decision as to the best type of advertising for the allotted dollars will be easier to make.

There are three basic types of advertising that you will be most interested in during the first few years of your business.

Start-up Advertising

This includes your business cards and stationery, announcement flyers and brochures, and your initial ads in newspapers or other publications. At this point, your main focus will be on telling people where you are located and what you can offer them.

Ongoing Advertising

Once the business is up and running, it will be vital to your success to institute a regular advertising campaign that is well thought out and—this is the key—consistent. Your goal at this point is to attract new clients, obtain repeat business from existing customers, and enhance your reputation.

Appearance Advertising

After you have reached the point where your business is on steady ground and you're showing increased profits every year, you can afford to dabble in "institutional advertising," as it is called in the trade. This is where you pick up the tab to send a dozen kids to the rodeo when it comes to town, or you sponsor a float in the local parade and, in return, get your name listed on the program or on a banner in the parade. This is primarily name recognition only and, while every little bit is helpful, by the time you can afford it, you probably will be in pretty good shape anyway.

Advertising Your Mail Order Business

The most effective means of advertising for the new mail order business is to run classified ads in newspapers and magazines. This is one of the easiest and most effective ways to advertise and is, overall, the least expensive of the various paid promotional techniques available.

Study the classifieds in your local newspaper, favorite consumer magazines, and point-of-purchase tabloids such as *The National Enquirer*. Examine the mail order ads and review how the product descriptions are written. Also check whether the reader is asked to send money for the product or must write for additional information.

The latter request is referred to as two-step marketing. When the inquiries for further information come in, a direct-mail sales kit is sent out that includes product brochures or a catalog, a sales letter (personalized by you; the company president), an order form, business reply envelope, and any other details you want to include such as user testimonials, discount or bonus offers, and guarantees—all of which serve to increase sales.

Classified Advertising

Classified ads can be crucial to business revenue—an inexpensive way to sell your service and hire employees. Don't underestimate the power of classified ads. Many major corporations use the

classifieds even though they have sizable budgets available for display advertising. There are several reasons for this.

1. The classifieds are an extremely reliable testing ground for new products, services, and ideas. Although it is true that people who typically read the classifieds are a different group from those who scan display ads, they are considered to be responsive and, therefore, can give you a very good idea of whether or not you have placed your ad in the appropriate publication.

2. A short, well-written classified placed in the right publication and under the proper category can be a low-cost method of advertising that guarantees solid returns.

3. If a company is trying to establish a mailing list, a classified ad that features an "Inquiry" statement, such as "Send name and address for free details (or a brochure)," is a good way to build up a file of qualified buyers' names. And they can be considered qualified buyers because it takes time, energy, and the cost of a postage stamp for them to get your free information. By writing to you they have stated their interest.

4. Classified ads are inexpensive, ranging from $0.50 cents to $15.00 per word, depending on the publication. With careful planning, you should be able to get broad-based coverage without putting a dent in your operating capital.

Sample Classified Advertisements

> FREE 100 DIET TIPS. Order your one-year subscription to Fight Flab Newsletter and receive revolutionary diet tips. Send $8.50 to FFN-A, P.O. Box 111, Anytown,USA 11111 or call (800) 555-5555.

> Make Money With Needed Products! Have you ever considered how many pet owners there are in America today? Millions of people spend billions of dollars every year on products for their pets. Find out about the most revolutionary pet product available. Send for free info: Pets, P.O. Box 11, Small Town, USA 11111.

When writing a classified ad it's necessary to get as much information in as small a space as possible. Since there is usually no art and your ad will be surrounded by many others, you must catch the reader's eye with the first few words. Therefore, you must make them as exciting as possible.

Use persuasive words that grab the reader's attention. Powerful persuaders include such words as save, earn, free, secret, learn, how to, success, love, or power. There are others that you will pick up by studying the classifieds.

It always helps to capitalize these lead words or to have them set in bold type. Some newspapers and magazines offer their advertisers large check marks, stars, or other grabbers to incorporate into the ad for a small charge.

Advertising is the greatest art form of the 20th Century.
 Marshall McLuhan

In the preceding sample classified ad ("Free! 100 Diet Tips"), note the FFN-A of the address. The "A" is a *key code* for the advertiser to determine how many responses are received from a particular publication. If the ad were to be run in a number of different places, the advertiser would insert a different key code for each placement to see which one was pulling the best response.

This is also useful if you're trying out a series of ads with slightly different copy treatment. By keying each one, you can tell which is the most effective. You can key the ad in a variety of ways. In addition to the method above (name-letter), you can use

a department number (e.g., FFN, Dept. 77). Or devise a method of your own.

The major step in keying ads is to maintain careful records. Your efforts won't amount to much if you forget to take advantage of this testing tool or tracking system. Whether you decide to use the record-keeping suggested earlier or come up with your own methods, just be sure to make a column to track key codes.

In terms of where to run classified ads, you should go the library, the local newsstand, or the magazine rack at the supermarket and look at different magazines. Some of the best include the following:

- ♦ American Home
- ♦ Better Homes and Gardens
- ♦ Capper's Weekly
- ♦ Extra Income
- ♦ Field & Stream
- ♦ Flower & Garden Magazine
- ♦ Grit
- ♦ House Beautiful
- ♦ Workbasket

As you can well imagine, there are more magazines, newspapers, and periodicals out there than you could ever use. You'll soon come to know the ones that work for you.

Display Advertising

Don't dismiss the possibility of running small display ads, even though they are more expensive than classified advertising, on a seasonal basis. Focus on promoting through display advertising during specific times of the year when you know that certain markets will need them.

As with all types of advertising, it is important to define your market when getting ready to place a display ad. Your main goal is to select a publication that will reach the audience you want,

then create a specific, attention-getting ad that appeals to that target group.

To Write or Not to Write

Writing display ad copy is not for the inexperienced. Although it is possible to learn how to put ideas and words together that will pull the results you desire, it is recommended that you hire a copywriter if you have any qualms about producing an ad.

However, if you are confident that you can develop your own ad, remember that it must build identity through the use of carefully planned words and design. Glance through newspapers and magazines to find ads that catch your eye. Most likely, the ones that stand out have a memorable logo, effective use of space, or an unusual headline that leads you into the body of the ad.

These are ads you should refer to as samples when designing your own.

When planning your ad, keep the following elements in mind:

1. *Visibility.* Your ad may be surrounded by many others, so design it so that it will immediately attract the reader's attention.

2. *Boldness.* Use large art and/or a bold headline as a focal point.

3. *Simplicity.* Don't overwhelm the reader with too many fine details. The ad's main point is lost and so is the reader's attention. This is particularly true in a small ad.

4. *White space.* Just because you have, say, a four-by-six-inch space to work with, it isn't necessary to fill it up. In fact, white space is a necessary component in assuring your ad will be read.

5. *Use simple-to-read typefaces.* Two that are popular are Times Roman and Bookman, which are known as serif typefaces because of the tiny strokes at the tops and bottoms of the letters.

 Sans-serif (without strokes) typefaces, such as Helvetica, are fine for ads containing only a few words,

but are difficult for the eye to follow when there is a lot of text.

Also, be sure that the type is large enough; generally nothing smaller than 10-point type should be used. If type is too small to read, it will simply be ignored.

Design and Typesetting

It isn't necessary to be a great artist to create an ad, especially these days with the availability of a variety of impressive graphic software programs. In addition, you can buy cut-out-and-transfer (press-on) letters in different typefaces, symbols, borders, and designs through graphic art supply companies. Most word processing programs also contain computer graphics that can dress up your ad at a low cost.

If you feel uncomfortable about laying out your ad so it has eye appeal, consider hiring an art student to handle the job for a prearranged fee or as a school assignment. (Talk with the head of the art department to see if there is a work/study for credit program.) Just be sure to review the student's work prior to making a commitment.

Also, check with the advertising department of the newspaper or magazine you are planning to advertise in. There may be graphic artists or designers on staff who will work on the layout for you. In fact, there are still newspapers in the country that offer full service, from ad concept to design work, at a minimal charge to their advertising clients.

Publications work on tight deadlines, so be sure you start the process early enough to get a proof copy of your ad back in time to make any corrections. You can imagine the anguish in seeing your ad appear with the wrong address. Although the publication would probably do a "make-good" for you and run a corrected ad at no charge, the damage has already been done. The final responsibility for the ad rests with you, so, as with any other aspect of your business, plan ahead.

Producing Your Own Catalog

These days, to be truly competitive in the world of mail order, it is almost imperative that your products be presented to potential customers in a catalog or, at bare minimum, a professional-looking product sheet.

There are basically two ways to approach the catalog issue. One is to design and produce a mail order catalog that includes all of the items you are promoting. The other method is to have your product or products included in an established catalog and pay a percentage of your sales for the opportunity. We will look at the pros and cons of each option.

The major drawbacks of creating a catalog to the beginning mail order business owner are the cost and the need to develop a focused product line. Mail order has become very specialized, with companies dealing only in a certain kind of clothing or specific types of pet products, kitchen equipment and supplies, household items, or health products, to name a few. With more than ten billion catalogs (and growing) filling the postal system every year, your catalog must have pizzazz if it is going to attract attention.

This calls for a catalog that includes the following:

1. An exciting cover that conveys an idea of what's inside

2. Inviting photographs or drawings of products

3. High-quality, straightforward copy describing the products and the philosophy and standards of your company

4. A unique layout that keeps the reader interested

5. An easy-to-follow, simple-to-use order form page

6. Top-quality printing that presents a polished, professional image

Naturally, this is an expensive proposition. You can figure on spending a minimum of $50,000 for a 2-color, 16-page catalog with a print run of approximately 100,000. Prices will vary according to the region, the kind of paper stock used, color versus black-and-white photography, and production costs for photographers, typesetting, copywriters, and designers. Even on the low

end, the Direct Marketing Association estimates that catalogs cost about $1,000 per page to produce.

You will need 100,000 catalogs to make the exercise worthwhile, based on initial response rates 1 percent to an exceptional 4 percent. In addition, there is the expense of warehousing a full inventory of fifty to seventy-five products, as well as packaging and shipping. Then you must figure on buying mailing lists that will provide you with samplings of solid prospect names. For the sake of discussion, count on spending between $35 and $60 for every 1,000 qualified buyers' names. The other major expense of producing your own catalog is postage, which will average about fifteen cents on a second class mailing.

With more than 10 billion catalogs in circulation, it is important that yours be exciting and targeted to an audience that will buy your products based on visual appeal.

As you can see, while producing your own catalog gives you absolute control over the way products are presented, the expense involved with production and mailing is so high that it would probably take you two years to recoup the cost. Therefore, this method is recommended only if you have a guaranteed top-selling line of products, a secure position in the market, and a captive and responsive audience.

Some mail order firms have found a way to reduce the expense and even realize a profit on their catalogs. By charging anywhere from $1 to $5, which is often credited to the first purchase, they are able to lessen the burden. However, the only way to ensure that customers will pay the price to receive your catalog is to be established, offer something unusual in the content, or gear your advertising campaign to a select market.

Product Sheets

It is possible to produce a good-looking product sheet of one to four pages for a lot less than you would spend on a catalog. Many mail order distributors dealing with only a few products have found this to be a viable alternative.

In most cases, you can have your typesetting done by a word processing service, which will reduce that expense from as much as $30 per page to $4 per page. Most word processing specialists should be able to follow your layout instructions and create a final copy that only requires you to paste in drawings or photographic halftones of your product.

If the copy is printed on a laser printer, it will be possible to get the sheets printed by a copy shop for approximately six to eight cents per page. And, because of the smaller size, postage will be much cheaper, especially if you have a bulk mailing permit. (Check with your local post office for details on bulk mailing.)

Again, however, the copy describing your product must be well written and easy for potential customers to understand. A concise order form incorporated into the product sheet will add convenience to the process for your customers.

Capitalizing on Established Catalogs

There are thousands of established catalogs you can use to get your products into the hands of the public. The advantages of exploring this option are the reduced expenses, since the design and production aspects are already taken care of, and the fact that the catalog already has a captive audience. Buyers for catalog companies are always looking for new products to offer their customers, and if you have something new and/or unique, chances are good that they would want to capitalize on it. This, in turn, can mean profits for you.

Finding the right catalogs for your product might be as easy as going through your own mail. If you have recently bought anything from a mail order house, you'll be on an "active" list that is purchased by a number of companies and should be receiving enough catalogs to have a representative sampling. There are catalogs for every hobby, interest, and lifestyle; some that may

even seem too narrow in scope to be profitable, so you must decide which one is best suited to your products.

A 16-page catalog will cost you approximately $1,000 per page to produce. A first-time response rate of 1 percent is considered average; 3 to 5 percent is considered a phenomenal success.

If you don't receive catalogs, there are a number of resource guides available at your local library that list mail order houses and their main areas of interest.

After you have a list of viable prospects, you must create a promotional package to send each. The package should include the following:

1. A cover letter with your name, address, telephone number, and professional affiliations (chamber of commerce, Better Business Bureau).

2. A product sheet with a detailed description, prices in varying quantities, discounts available to the mail order house (most expect a discount of approximately 60 to 65 percent off retail, which you will make up in volume), shipping details, and manufacturing capability.

3. A professional photograph of the product, showing applications for its use, if possible.

4. An offer to send a sample upon request. Large companies, such as L.L. Bean, which sends out more than seventy-five million catalogs a year, would not be able to handle the load if they accepted sample products. By following up with a telephone call several weeks after sending your promotional package, you will be advised whether or not the company wants to see a sample, or they will write and request one if interested.

If your product is turned down, have another look at the catalog to which you submitted information. Does your product really look

as if it would be a good fit with their merchandise mix? If you still think it is, you can resubmit your package at a later date in the event their needs change.

If, on the other hand, a mail order house accepts your product, they will send out a supplier form for you to fill out and probably submit an order to test the product in their catalog. Most will not expect you to give them exclusive rights unless the product is unbelievably special.

If it works, there is a possibility that other mail order houses will also want to work with you. Some may want to work with you on a drop ship basis so that when they receive an order, it is forwarded to you for filling, which reduces the discount amount you will be expected to extend.

Mail order catalog sales are increasing every year. Getting your products carried by an established mail order house can be a very profitable situation for you. So if start-up capital is a problem, be sure to investigate this extremely logical and workable option.

Taking Advantage of the Postal System

Direct mail advertising is the next most effective means of getting business. The phrase may not mean much to you, but you get direct-mail pieces all the time. You know those catalogs, brochures, or other solicitation materials you get in the mail almost daily from people you've never contacted? That's direct mail.

Since you haven't requested this information, you may throw it away without a second glance. However, if it's an attractive or unusual advertising piece, you will probably decide to look it over. Maybe something—a picture or catchy copy—will grab your eye and you will order a product from the company that mailed the material.

This is one example of direct mail; unsolicited advertising material that is mailed out to a large group of people. The addressees may be bound by any number of factors—credit card holders, members of an organization, the same ethnic group, age, occupation, or ZIP code. These and the names of people in thousands of other categories are accumulated, organized, and sold by mailing-list brokers for use in direct mail campaigns.

There are advantages to using direct mail when starting out, though the cost is too high for most people to use it in the beginning. The primary benefit is control. You can rent a mailing list that is made up of the names and addresses of very specific groups of people.

When you are selecting products to sell through mail order, you most likely have an idea about your ideal audience. Obviously, if you can reach these potential buyers, you will have a greater percentage of people reading your material than if you went with general mass advertising.

Mailing lists can be compiled by you as you gather names, or you can rent them from a list broker. Check in the library for volumes that list brokers in the areas you desire. You will find lists available for everything from folks who regularly donate blood to people who sent back a "no" response to magazine subscription renewal offers and hundreds of other seemingly obscure samplings.

However, obscure listings are often exactly what you need in the mail order business. If, for example, you were selling a unique type of guitar string, you can bet there would be a mail list of guitar owners.

List rental rates vary according to the popularity rate of the group and the number of names involved. Figure on spending between $35 to $50 per thousand names. Plan to test 5,000 to 10,000 names on a list to determine your product's appeal to that group.

Preparing Your Direct-Mail Package

What goes into the direct-mail package? A letter that is both a handshake to introduce yourself and a sales presentation. It can be a tough balance. Sales letters are the least expensive direct-mail pieces to produce, but they are far from the easiest to write. You may want to hire a copywriter to handle that task for best results. If you choose to write the letter yourself, bear in mind these points:

♦ The letter introduces your service to potential buyers.

♦ A dynamic lead-in sentence is essential.

♦ The benefits of dealing with you must be concise and clear.

- There should be a feeling of personal communication to the person who's reading it.
- It must be highly professional.

Think of what it takes to draw you into a direct-mail piece and keep you interested until the last word: a thought-provoking phrase in big, bold letters at the top of the page; a simple but thorough explanation of why the letter was being sent and how reading it would be of benefit to you; a direct request to take action; a few testimonials from the service's users; the signature of the company's president. All these factors should be considered when preparing your direct-mail sales letter.

Experiment with writing a letter, get some feedback from friends and associates—perhaps even test it locally—but make sure you're sending out something you truly believe will work for you. Not all letters will be as focused as the example above, but the elements remain the same.

If your letterhead does not contain it, include your name, title, and phone number. Shortly after your mailing, make a follow-up phone call if you have phone numbers available. If handled effectively, the combination of direct mail and phone follow-up can generate a great deal of business. You can generate all your direct-mail letters and merge them with your mailing list with various software programs. You will be amazed at how quickly and efficiently you can do work that would otherwise take hours, even days.

Predicting Ad Response

There is a standardized formula in advertising that provides a barometer for predicting how much response can be expected from either a display ad or a classified ad. The formula states that you will see one-half of the total responses from an ad within a certain period of time after receiving your first inquiry or order.

For an ad run in a daily newspaper, the period of time is three days; for a weekly newspaper or magazine, it is six days; within fifteen days for a monthly publication; and within twenty-five days when running in a bimonthly. Although there will be exceptions to this rule, it does give you a base from which to track response.

Determining Your Cost Per Thousand

The cost per thousand (CPM) equation helps you develop a cost-effective campaign. Basically, it tells you what your ad cost per thousand readers will be. Most publications will provide a CPM comparison upon request (some include it in their Media Kits), but you can figure it out for yourself with just a few facts from publications that you are exploring as advertising vehicles.

For convenience sake, CPM equations are typically based on the rate of a full-page, black-and-white ad. You simply divide the full-page rate by the thousands of circulation. It is important that you get the circulation, *not* the readership, because magazines and newspapers typically claim that their readership is 2 to 50 percent higher because of "pass-along" of the publication to friends or relatives.

For example, if a certain newspaper is charging $2,000 for a full-page ad and it claims the true circulation is 200,000, you will be paying $10 per 1,000 readers for your ad space. Another specialized publication's full-page rate may be $1,000 with a circulation of 50,000. The cost per 1,000 readers will be much higher—$20 per 1,000, but it might be worth it if, for example, you have a unique product or service that is geared to an exclusive market.

Benefits of Paid Circulation

It is also important to know that publications with a paid circulation generally have a readership that is more inclined to respond to advertising. This is because of the simple fact that they are a captive audience who have taken the time to *order* the publication. This is especially valuable if you have a product or service that you're planning to market through mail-order channels.

You can find circulation, readership demographics, advertising rates, and other important information about a number of publications (especially those with national distribution) through *Standard Rate and Data Service (SRDS)*, available through the research desk of your local library.

The Advertising Research Foundation and the Association of Business Publishers conducted a study to determine the impact of

advertising on the sale of products. Several different products were used for the study, and each was advertised for a twelve-month period in an appropriate publication. The results were interesting, but not surprising to anyone who has ever utilized a solid advertising campaign in promoting a business.

- ♦ More advertising meant more sales.

- ♦ Determining results from an ad campaign generally took four to six months. One or two insertions do not indicate viable results.

- ♦ Color in advertisements dramatically increased response and sales.

- ♦ A well-developed ad campaign keeps on working for a year and sometimes even longer in publications with high "keep" appeal.

Knowledge and belief in your product, faith in yourself, and respect for your customers are the keys to successfully building your future. As you go about starting and establishing your business, remember the word "profit." This alone should give you the necessary motivation to get out there and confidently tell the world what you have to offer.

Notes

Key Points

Personal Thoughts

Additional Research

21

PROMOTION AND PUBLIC RELATIONS

Informing the public about your business through the use of business cards, brochures, mailing pieces, catalogs, and specialty items, such as calendars, pens, and T-shirts imprinted with your company name, is known as *promotion.* What you do over and above your paid advertising and promotion that builds your image and keeps your business in the public consciousness is referred to as *public relations.* It is a fine line in terminology, but it can make or break your business if not addressed.

Some businesses promote by trying to make themselves more visible. An example of this would be the new fried chicken restaurant that has someone dressed in a chicken suit stand in front of the store to draw in customers. Other businesses give away premiums to increase the customer's sense of getting a good deal.

Obviously, mail order operations cannot make themselves more visible by wearing costumes. So they dress up their ads with giveaways or premium gifts with a minimum order. Readers seeing the words "FREE" or "FREE GIFT" will certainly have their interest in your enterprise stirred up. As a new operator you will most likely not be able to spend much money on elaborate promotions, but there are ways to promote inexpensively.

For example, to generate responses that you can use to mail back information about your product, make a one-page list of tips about anything. Go to the library and find ten to twenty tips on house hunting, college scholarships, accounting, whatever.

Write an ad geared to a specific market offering whatever it is you've chosen fee of charge, and ask the reader to send a self-addressed, stamped envelope (SASE). The SASE request will probably lower your response rate, but it will save you time and money. When responses come in, mail back photocopies of your tips, keeping a list of the names and addresses for sending out promotion pieces.

Keep It Simple

As your business grows, you'll want to learn more about how contests, sweepstakes, and premiums can be good promotional tools. But for the purposes of starting out in mail order, keep it simple. Test a number of promotions like the tips list. Try a crafts pattern or recipes. Once you get those leads in, you have a captive audience for your "bounce-back" materials.

In considering promotional efforts, keep these points in mind:

♦ The best time to promote is between September and November, when people shop by mail to ease holiday chores. The second best time is from January to April, when folks spend more time at home than during the summer months.

♦ Accept the philosophy of spending money to make money.

Getting Into Print and Television

Publicity is another way to get attention, though you won't find "free ads." To get media publicity—mentions in newspapers and magazines or on radio and television—you need to approach outlets as a source of information that will benefit that medium's audience versus as someone trying to sell goods.

Many publications have new product sections, for example. Or you might be able to get mention as a new business in certain publications. But rarely, if ever, will you find the opportunity to

sell through free publicity, because editors will see through any efforts to advertise in a press release.

Should you decide to write up a press release and do a targeted publicity mailing, bear in mind that there are four main reasons why editors throw away releases.

1. Some releases are just thinly disguised commercial advertising, offering no news or information of value to the editor and his or her audience.

2. Some releases are adequate enough in their content and writing but are sent to inappropriate prospects or are sent at the wrong time.

3. Some releases are scheduled for use but get bumped when something deemed more important comes along.

4. Seasonal material must go out at the right time; remember that most publications work months ahead. If a seasonal release is received at the wrong time, it will be trashed.

There is a standard format for press releases. See the example on the following page for a company that sells how-to genealogy books.

There are no guarantees that your press release will get you any publicity, but it's worth a try. Just make sure you target the release to an appropriate publication and the proper editor; in this case, the features editor would be a good bet.

Keeping Motivation High

The justification for investing in advertising and promotion is time. If you attempted to contact all of the people who read ads and press release materials in newspapers and magazines or those who listen to the radio or watch television, you would never have time to conduct your business, you would be too busy recruiting.

Sample Press Release

For immediate release For more imformation:
(Your name and phone #)

CLIMB YOUR FAMILY TREE

Genealogy is fast becoming a popular pasttime for Americans who show a growing interest in learning about their roots. Researching the family tree takes a great deal of time and effort, however, and not knowing the right methods can make the whole experience frustrating.

Experts in the field say that taking the time to learn proper research techniques can make a significant difference in results.

A free list of research techniques from Genealogical Services is available by sending a self-addressed, stamped envelope to

Genealogical services, P.O. Box 1234
Anytown, USA 11111

Advertisements contain the only truths to be relied on in a newspaper.

Thomas Jefferson

Time is money! As a small business owner, you will want to devote as much attention as possible to the production end of your venture and let your advertising and promotion work bring in customers.

Knowledge and belief in your product, faith in yourself, and respect for your customers are the keys to successfully building your future. As you go about starting up and establishing your business, remember the word "profit." This alone should give you the necessary motivation to get out there and confidently tell the world what you have to offer.

There are many clever ways to extend the effectiveness of your advertising and promotional dollars, as illustrated in the following examples.

Charity Tie-ins

Other ideas you might consider include promoting humanitarian outreach. For example, for every ten products a customer buys or every tenth time a customer orders from you, you donate a predetermined amount of money to a local charity.

Giveaways

According to successful entrepreneurs, free giveaways are the most successful promotions. You can order items such as pens, pencils, notepads, and calendars with your name and phone number printed on them. Every time the recipient uses the item, he or she will automatically think of you! Check under "Advertising Specialties" in the Yellow Pages for prices and ideas.

Reminder Cards

Send regular "thanks for your business" cards to your clientele.

Customer Service

One of the most overlooked areas in promoting business is the way we create an impression when dealing with the public on a one-to-one basis. The ageless philosophy that the customer is always right and comes first has, it seems, gotten lost in the shuffle in these days of fast-paced transactions.

As a small business owner, you can be sure that customers will flock to you if you make them feel important. It is as easy as greeting them warmly on the telephone (instruct your employees, if you have them, to do the same), maintaining a courteous attitude, and inviting them to order soon—even if they have not spent any money. Send regular "thanks-for-your-business" cards to your clientele. Remember that word travels fast, and if you create an atmosphere that makes all your customers feel special, you can be sure they will tell their friends and neighbors.

Getting Started

At this point, you're ready to give the mail order business a try. If you've done your homework, by now you should know

◆ The products you plan to sell

◆ What your prices will be for the products

◆ Your start-up costs and equipment needs

◆ Where you will work—most likely home—and how to set up the space

◆ How to get started with advertising and promotion

It is absolutely crucial that you approach your start-up with good planning and organization. Take each step knowing what the previous step was and which step comes next. Likewise, know what you want to happen and what could happen; plan for problems, and have possible solutions ready.

This book just scratches the surface of the knowledge that you will want—and need—to acquire in the course of starting your business and making it grow. There are many resources to help you learn and stay abreast of the industry's latest news. Some of these resources follow in the Appendix.

In closing, there are several points about you and your success in a mail order business that bear repeating:

1. Don't expect to succeed overnight. This can only serve to discourage you while things are slow.

2. Maintain a "customer first" orientation. It will ensure repeat business and customer referrals.

3. The mail order business is booming. With the right amount of effort and entrepreneurship, your ride on the wave can be quite comfortable.

Good luck to you in your new endeavor.

Notes

Key Points

Personal Thoughts

Additional Research

22

TRADE TERMINOLOGY

As with any business, there is language peculiar to mail order that you'll want to be familiar with for your day-to-day operations. Knowing the lingo can be of tremendous value when establishing business relationships, and it is particularly helpful when dealing with problems. Here is a brief list of some common words and phrases you'll encounter:

ARO (After Receipt of Order). Used to indicate specific time after an order is received when it will be delivered.

Bulk Mail. A category of third-class mail for advertising/circular material. Use requires minimum quantities of 200 pieces, or by the pound, and a permit

Business Reply Mail. Where the addressee (you) guarantee postage costs. Requires a permit. Using this makes customer replies easy and will usually guarantee high response rates.

Cleaning. Where a mailing list is tested to eliminate unusable names.

Column Inch. Refers to ad space one inch high by one column width. Space ad rates are computed by this unit of measurement.

Copy. Advertising text.

Copyright. Status granted by law that establishes ownership and certain rights relating to published work.

Dead Names. Names invalidated because person no longer lives at the address on the mailing list.

Direct Mail. Where advertising is sent directly to prospective buyers, either requested or from a list.

Drop Ship. Where you give a manufacturer names and payment, and the product is shipped to customers under your name, or an arrangement with a mail order house that includes your product in its catalog and mails orders to you to be filled.

Envelope Stuffers. Material enclosed in envelopes and sent to established or prospective customers (also Insert).

EOM (End of Month). On invoices and quotations, indicates when payment is requested.

Insertion. When your ad appears in a publication (results from an *insertion order*).

Key or Key Code. Used to track ad responses to the publication in which the ad appeared.

Lazy Words. Words that do not contribute to the reader getting the sales presentation.

Line Rate. How much a periodical charges for a line in an ad.

List Broker. Someone in the business of procuring and making available mailing lists. Buys, sells, and leases names.

Mailing List. A list from which you draw names and addresses of prospective customers, used for direct-mail efforts.

Market Research. A formal or informal study of how well the public will receive a product or service.

Media. All the sources you can utilize for advertising: magazines, newspapers, radio, television, posters, packaging, etc.

Merchandising. Covers all aspects of preparing, promoting, and presenting a product or service to prospective customers.

Novelty Item. Something different or unusual, often a "fun" product.

Optimum Price. Selling price that produces the highest net profit.

Overhead. All your business expenses.

Second Chance Offer. Sent to a potential customer who didn't order the first time around.

Self-Mailer. A mailing piece that can be sent without an envelope; generally three-folded with an address label.

Testimonial. Words of praise from a satisfied customer, used in advertising.

Tickler. File used to regulate work flow, set up by days of the month or week.

Tie-in. A side product or service marketed in association with the main product or service.

There are other words and phrases you'll come across in the course of doing business, talking with advertising representatives, and dealing with printers. Don't assume what someone means when they use a word or phrase that is not familiar. Ask for a definition in layman's terms. You'll find that speaking the language makes the job a lot easier.

APPENDIX: RESOURCES

Associations and Agencies

Small Business Associations & Government Agencies

American Marketing Association
250 South Wacker Drive, Suite 200
Chicago, IL 60606-5819

Marketing publications available to nonmembers.

Bureau of the Census
Washington, DC 20233

Statistical data on such topics as retail/wholesale trade, manufacturers, service industries, transportation, etc.

Chambers of Commerce
Consult Yellow Pages. Services vary among chambers but may include advice, support, workshops or seminars, local business news, and other services specifically for small businesses.

Council of Better Business Bureaus
4200 Wilson Boulevard, Suite 800
Arlington, VA 22203

Ask for a listing of their "Booklets on Wise Buying."

Dun & Bradstreet
299 Park Avenue
New York, NY 10171

Send for the booklet "This is Dun & Bradstreet," an overview of publications and services.

Internal Revenue Service (IRS)
1-800-829-1040 General tax assistance
1-800-829-3676 Forms and publications

See the government section of your phone book for address and phone number of the local office. The IRS publishes a variety of books and brochures that are useful to owners of small businesses. Each year the IRS publishes *Tax Guide for Small Business.*

International Franchise Association
1350 New York Avenue NW
Washington, DC 20005

Regulation and information on franchises.

Local Planning Agencies
See the government section of your phone book for address and phone number of the local office. Source of information on zoning and future development locations.

Minority Business Development Agency
Office of Public Affairs
Department of Commerce
Washington, DC 20230

National Association for the Self-Employed
PO Box 612067
DFW Airport, TX 75261-2067

National Association of Women Business Owners
600 South Federal Street
Chicago, IL 60605

National Federation of Independent Business
150 West 20th Avenue
San Mateo, CA 94403

National Insurance Consumer Organization
PO Box 3243
Merrifield, VA 22116-3243

Send $3 and self-addressed, stamped #10 envelope for booklet, "Buyer's Guide to Insurance."

National Minority Business Council
235 East 42nd Street
New York, NY 10017

Bimonthly newsletter for small and minority businesses.

National Small Business United
1155 15th Street NW, Suite 710
Washington, DC 20005

Send for information on federal legislation.

Occupational Safety & Health Administration (OSHA)
Department of Labor
200 Constitution Avenue NW
Washington, DC 20210

Employment regulations.

Office of Information and Public Affairs
U.S. Department of Labor
200 Constitution Avenue NW
Washington, DC 20210

Request publications list regarding employment.

Service Corps of Retired Executives (SCORE)
See Small Business Administration.

Small Business Administration
1441 L Street NW
Washington, DC 20416

The SBA is the primary source of federal governmental assistance for small businesses. In addition to providing financing for many small businesses, it provides a number of services for free or at a small cost. SBA regional offices routinely conduct free or low-cost small business workshops. The SBA also offers many helpful publications as well as the following hotlines:

SBA Answer Desk
Recorded information on a variety of topics

1-800-827-5722

SBA Online
A national electronic bulletin board service that provides an overview of SBA information.

1-800-859-INFO if you use a 2400 baud modem or 800-697-INFO if you use a 9600 baud modem

See also following entry.

Service Corps of Retired Executives (SCORE)
PO Box 15434
Fort Worth, TX 76119

Retired business executives offer their expertise and services to entrepreneurs through SBA's SCORE, which charges for out-of-pocket expenses but not for the consultant's time.

Telephone Company
Consult your local phone company. Most offer a variety of services and publications for small businesses.

AT&T 800-Number Information
Call 1-800-272-0400.

Trade

Direct Marketing Association, Inc.
11 West 42nd Street, 25th Floor
New York, NY 10036

Books

General Reference Books & Periodicals

Note: Many of the following resources are available through the Research Desk at your local library.

A Consumer's Guide to Telephone Service
Consumer Information Center, Pueblo, CO 81009

Bacon's Newspaper/Magazine Directory
A comprehensive listing of every major newspaper and magazine in the United States and Canada.

Directory of Publications and Broadcast Media
Published annually by Gale Research Company, Detroit, MI.

The Dun & Bradstreet Middle Market Directory and
The Dun & Bradstreet Million Dollar Directory
The Dun & Bradstreet Corporation, New York, NY

Encyclopedia of Associations
Published annually by Gale Research Company, Detroit, MI.

Encyclopedia of Business Information Sources
Published periodically by Gale Research Company, Detroit, MI.

Financial Studies of the Small Business
Financial Research Associates
PO Box 7708
Winter Haven, FL 33883

National Five-Digit ZIP Directory (2 volumes)
U.S. Postal Service
6060 Primacy Parkway, Suite 101
Memphis, TN 38188-0001.

Also available by phone 1-800-238-3150 or through your local post office.

Poor's Register of Corporations, Directors, and Executives
New York, NY: Standard & Poor's Corporation

Roget's Thesaurus in Dictionary Form
New York: HarperCollins, 1992

Synonyms and antonyms.

Tax Guide for Small Businesses
Internal Revenue Service publication. Published annually. Available from local IRS office.

Thomas Register of American Manufacturers
Thomas Publishing Company, New York, NY

Ulrich's International Periodicals Directory
Comprehensive listing of major magazines and newspapers.

Webster's New Collegiate Dictionary
Springfield, MA: G & C Merriam Company, 1989

Where to Find Business Information
by David Brownstone and Gorton Carruth

New York: John Wiley & Sons, 1982

Trade

Note: There are a substantial number of titles written for specific products and/or businesses; see your local bookseller or library for the titles that pertain to your specialty. A few representative examples have been included.

Mail Order & Catalog Shopping
By American Business Directories Staff
Omaha, NE: American Business Directories, 1992

Mail Order Business Directory
Coral Springs, FL: B. Klein Publications, 1992

Mail Order Foreign Bargains Directory
New York, NY: Gordon Press, 1987

Mail Order Legal Manual
by Erwin J. Keup

Grants Pass, OR: Oasis Press, 1990

Mail Order Product Guide
by Barry T. Klein

Scottsdale, AZ: Todd Publishing, 1993

Mail Order Shopper for Parents
by Hal Morgan

New York, NY: Doubleday, 1990

United States Mail Order Industry
by Maxwell Sroge

Homewood, IL: BusinessOne Irwin, 1991

Magazines

Catalogs of Products and Supplies

Dellware
Dell Direct Sale L.P.
11209 Metric Boulevard
Austin, TX 78758-4093

Global Computer Supplies
2318 East Del Amo Boulevard, Department 43
Compton, CA 90220
1-800-845-6225

MacWarehouse
PO Box 3013
1720 Oak Street
Lakewood, NJ 08701-3013
1-800-255-6227

PaperDirect, Inc.
PO Box 677
205 Chubb Avenue
Lyndhurst, NJ 07071-0677
1-800-272-7377

Viking Office Products
Six locations nationwide
1-800-421-1222

General Business

Business Marketing
Crain Communications, Inc.
740 N. Rush Street
Chicago, IL 60611

Published monthly.

Entrepreneur Magazine
2392 Morse Avenue
Irvine, CA 92714

Published monthly.

Sales & Marketing Management
Bill Communications, Inc.
355 Park Avenue South
New York, NY 10010

Published monthly except in June, August, and October, when it is published twice a month.

Success, The Magazine for Today's Entrepreneurial Mind

Lang Communications
230 Park Avenue
New York, NY 10169

Published monthly with the exception of bimonthly issues for January/February and July/August.

Working Woman

Lang Communications
230 Park Avenue
7th Floor
New York, NY 10169

Published monthly.

Trade

The Competitive Advantage

1901 NW 23rd Avenue
Portland, OR 97210

Monthly that includes ideas for improving sales, marketing, and management practices.

Mail Order Entrepreneur

PO Box 14689
Dayton, OH 45413

Published eight times a year and covers new products and industry news.

Money-Making Opportunities

11071 Ventura Boulevard
Studio City, CA 91604

Published eight times a year. Features new products.

Opportunity

73 Spring Street
New York, NY 10012

Monthly with emphasis on direct selling/merchandising and financial survival tips for independent businesspeople. Features include sales techniques, new products, salepeople profiles, special event sales news.

Successful Meetings Magazine
633 Third Avenue
New York, NY 10017

Monthly listing of trade shows.

Index